passion for **speed**

passion for **speed**

Twenty-four classic cars that
shaped a century of motor sport

Nick Mason and Mark Hales

CARLTON
BOOKS

To my father, Bill Mason, who got me into all this,
and to my mother for allowing him to.

Nick Mason

To Terry Grimwood, who got me started,
but has probably forgotten.

Mark Hales

This revised and updated edition published
in 2010 by Carlton Books Limited
20 Mortimer Street
London W1T 3JW

First published in 1998 by Virgin Books

A catalogue record for this title is available from the British Library

ISBN 978 1 84732 639 3

Art direction and design: The Team
Julian Grice, Adrian Mewett and David Richards
Publishing consultant: Philip Dodd
Editorial support: John Dabbs, Mike Hallowes and Diana Vowles
Production management: The Foundry Design And Production

Printed and bound in China

When we set out to create the first edition of this book, we were fairly sure that nothing like it had ever been attempted before. There had been plenty of track tests in magazines and the odd performance test against the clock, but rarely both together and certainly not on the scale we were contemplating. There had been plenty of history too. After all, these cars had already been driven by some of the greatest drivers ever.

For this third edition we have added a further two chapters, featuring the striking Ferrari Enzo and, at the opposite end of the automotive spectrum, the delightful little Alfa Romeo TZ. Throughout we have remained true to the original objectives. First, we wanted to sit the reader in the driving seat. We also wanted to tell the story of how the cars were discovered and acquired and what they were like to own as well as to drive. And we both wanted to see how the performance of the older cars compared with more modern machinery.

The main thing, though, was to enjoy ourselves. We have managed to do that for a great deal longer than we expected, and we hope it still shows.

I generally try and avoid using the word 'collection' to describe the cars I own. It sounds too deliberate, too passionless.

Like a lot of people who buy old cars, I've ended up with an idiosyncratic (with an emphasis on the 'idio') mix of models which reflect my own personal enthusiasms. There's not much point in collecting just one marque, because all manufacturers - even Ferrari - made some less than great cars alongside their classics.

My passion for cars and motor racing predates any involvement with music. My father, a director for Shell's documentary film unit, used to take me in his four and a half litre Bentley to the vintage car events he was competing in, and some of my happiest childhood memories include the smell of leather, hot oil and blended racing fuels, accompanying the ticking sound of hot metal. From that introduction, I was set on a course towards wanting to race cars for fun, particularly old ones, although fortunately I never had the ambition, or delusion, of being the Graham or Damon Hill of my day.

One of the joys of motor racing is the split between the lonely responsibility of being at the wheel in a race - you can't have a band meeting as you go into a difficult corner - and the dry-humoured camaraderie of the paddock. There is an extraordinary willingness amongst fellow competitors and team mechanics to share experiences, jokes, knowledge and spare parts. It's a world I love being part of, and my membership of the British Racing Drivers Club is an achievement that I am particularly proud of.

It is even possible to become friends with some of the dealers, despite the relationship of hunter and hunted that inevitably exists between us. I respect their ability to trail some tempting bait across my path, patiently waiting for it to be taken. And off they go, laughing merrily all the way to the bank, the kinder ones buying me a drink from the profits.

Buying old cars is a risky investment. Prices have roller-coastered alarmingly over the last thirty years or so: the Ferrari 250GTO, which I bought for £35,000 in 1973 suddenly soared, during the boom of the 1980s, to £10 million in 1987 before plunging back down. I was once invited to appear on a financial TV programme as an investment expert. By the time the recording was due to take place, car values had plummeted and I was promptly uninvited.

If the fluctuations of the market are erratic, there is one safe bet in owning old cars. The re-builds will rarely, if ever, come in below budget or on time. The cars are so individual that replacement parts have to be specially sourced or more often hand-made. It may then seem particularly odd to risk all this work on the road, let alone the track. Unfortunately for my own pulse rate and cheque book I find that although many of these cars are extremely elegant at rest, they only achieve their true beauty in motion, being driven somewhere near the limit of their potential. Stuffed tigers are all very well, but no substitute for the version in the wild. Graceful in motion and capable of delivering a really nasty bite.

Sadly my taste in choosing cars has not always been impeccable. For a while I was looking hard for a mid-1950s Indianapolis car. I tracked one down and restored it. But on the track it was terrifying: only two gears, an extraordinary driving position, poor suspension and brakes that would fail any M.o.T. test. I later discovered that Fangio had refused to drive the same car after a number of practice laps, so I felt I was in good company. On the other hand, the Maserati Birdcage was love at first gear - I hadn't driven one before I bought it, so I was unprepared for the treat of sitting behind the wheel. There are no excuses offered for the older cars: races in the pre-war Aston or ERA can be just as exciting as competing at Le Mans.

Of course it's fun to see people enjoy the cars, although sometimes it's alarming to see the abandon with which grown men drape themselves over a car bonnet to drool over the bodywork. However, I have to confess I'm not totally selfless - most of the pleasure has been personal.

Nick Mason, London, 2010

My contribution to these pages has been a great deal easier because of Nick's laid-back attitude. It is now over twenty years since I first met him for a test of his newly acquired Ferrari F40 at Donington Park only to see him disappear in search of coffee rather than watch me at work. A few years later when a freezing damp track caught me out and I hit the wall with his Tyrrell, he barely averted his gaze from the financial pages. When I needed a second or even a third day to try the McLaren, and then the Enzo, on a dry road, he was busy elsewhere so we just got on with it.

None of this is affected; it's all completely genuine. The fact that a lifetime behind a drum kit has given Nick the means to mend the Tyrrell, and to buy the F40 or Enzo, is irrelevant. There aren't many people like him. We might have managed to produce a book about someone else's collection, but it is doubtful whether it would have been such a relaxed and enjoyable affair.

Mark Hales

Over the years I have driven more than a few cars. I did it the hard way at first, toiling either side of the paying job, patching up some tired machine in the hope it would last ten laps of Brands Hatch. It got better and so did I, until people more skilled than I were preparing and I was driving.

In the meantime I took up writing until that became my trade. In turn that opened a few doors and this book was one of the more significant ones. I am now more grateful than ever that I served an apprenticeship, because understanding the machinery better equips you to drive it. I was also aware how difficult and time consuming it is to ensure cars make the finish.

I could never have imagined, though, as I trailed my Sunbeam Tiger to Croft Autodrome in the early 70s, that I would add the contents of this book to my personal list. Cars like the ERA and the Bugatti are so rare and so valuable that only a select few ever get to drive them. That I should be tasked with driving them so hard was an added, yet more exclusive bonus. And then there was the 250F. The fulfilment of a dream, the end of an almost lifelong quest. There was the Birdcage Maserati about which I knew little but which made every single corner the most fun I can remember in years. The Lotus 18 Formula 1 which ushered in the mid-engined revolution, the Lola sports racer from a time when sports cars had enough of tradition and enough new technology to be the best of both worlds.

There were others like the GTO where it was better to affect the detached air of the professional racer lest I dwelt on how much it would cost to replace, but whose personality cut through all that within a lap. There was the 962 Porsche whose massive grip and huge power were more familiar. This, however, was the model that won Le Mans more times than any other and it was fascinating to see how. And the more recent additions in the shape of the McLaren and Enzo have provided an intriguing footnote to this automotive tapestry. Their technology is more modern, certainly, but not necessarily any more accessible. There was the feeling that race and road cars had finally evolved into separate breeds and the very idea of driving your race car to Le Mans and back again was no more than a quirk of history.

It only reaffirmed the feeling I had when we finished the first edition. That the cars were players in a glorious age that has slipped away. Not everything old is necessarily better than what we have today, but the time when the joy of competition was an end in itself and where car and engine designers ploughed their own

For the purposes of this book it was vital that all the cars had an equal chance to show themselves to their best advantage. I may have driven them all, but there are still some cars that have me inventing excuses before I even climb aboard. Mark was someone who could drive them to the limit, and who was experienced and flexible enough to make the necessary mental adjustments between drives.

I knew he could drive from a car magazine session with the F40 in the wet at Donington, which had me retreating to the motorhome while Mark headed purposefully toward the car. And he wasn't just brave, he was quick too. Also, since this book was his idea as well as mine, it would have been very bad manners to look for anyone else.

Nick Mason

Mark Hales

stylistic furrow are good things which have probably gone forever. So are treaded racing tyres. Wings and slicks were well established by the time I started racing and although the many historic festivals celebrate motorsport's history and keep it alive, whole generations of drivers brought up on modern machinery have no idea of the sheer pleasure available from cars uncorrupted by technology. Cars like the 250F had significant power but little grip and no aerodynamic aids. Driving one was like handling a more modern car on a permanently wet road. To research the forgotten techniques like the four-wheel drift and the deliberate power slide, to experience the precision of a GTO's steering, were sheer delights not available anywhere else these days.

The tactile pleasure of narrow, treaded tyres and the thrill of endless powerslides are guilty pleasures I continue to cherish every year, but there had to be a serious side if we were to bring all this indulgence to the reader. More than anything I wanted to convey the physical sensation of driving these cars, the part usually missing from a track test. If I have concentrated too much on the technique, then so be it. I couldn't think of a better way to sit you in the seat. Neither do I make any apologies for the extensive use of musical analogies. Conformity of purpose and the pursuit of optimum engineering efficiency has all but snuffed out variety in engine design, and the sound an engine makes is no longer its unique signature. It is almost impossible to tell whose name is on the cam covers by just listening. Music, and the instruments that generate it, are part of everybody's lives and I can think of no better way to bring the car alive on the page.

Mark Hales, Conisholme, Lincolnshire, April 2010

We soon learnt to expect no sympathy for the problems in testing such a range of cars, but consider these details.

Silverstone is one of the busiest tracks in Britain, so most of our testing and photography had to be done during the British winter. A wet track makes lap times meaningless, and freezing cold renders wide, treadless slick tyres impotent to the point where they are lethal. Winter winds might freeze the assembled company to the core but they also make sound recording difficult, while vintage magneto ignitions have a spark lively enough to phase anything containing modern electronics. The spikes from BRM, ERA and Bugatti magnetos dealt various lethal blows to Datron's space-age speed measuring equipment and to Captain Cacophony's Digital Audio Tape recorders, while sparks from any of the Ferraris seemed to afflict everything.

We don't expect anyone to sympathise, but operating racing cars is an activity best reserved for the summer months. Even when there isn't a technical problem as such, their engines are simply not designed to run in freezing cold. None of them liked starting in the first place and when they finally did, the oil rarely reached a temperature where it can do its best work without large amounts of tape over the radiators. Methanol fuel freezes in an engine's inlets so the awesome supercharged V16 engine in the BRM stood no chance whatever of completing a lap. Added to which, getting a large number of cars to a circuit to coincide neatly with the wildest, coldest weather the UK had seen for many a decade, then fitting in at least 65 acceleration runs, 230 timed laps, 400 familiarisation laps, 450 recording laps and some 10,000 pictures, at two different tracks, was not an easy piece of logistics.

The weather and the BRM eventually defeated us in year one so we had to wait exactly 12 months until the circuit was free again. And wouldn't you know it, the weather did exactly the same. Same date, different year but right on cue, closely followed by a repeat performance from the BRM. The McLaren chapter needed several attempts, although in that case the rain did enhance the photography if not the driving experience. Bang on cue, six years later, the Enzo was splashing round a wet Anglesey. Fortunately, the British climate's capricious nature does also allow it to change for the better, but that we succeeded in producing this book the way we wanted is part evidence of the race mechanic's spirit, and part testament to Nick Mason's insistence that we stick to our original plan.

It is now yours to read, to look at and to listen to.

Sound recording equipment list
Tape machines
4 x Sony PDR.1000 TC Portadat recorders
1 x Casio DA.7 portable DAT recorder
1 x Sony TCD C8 MiniDat recorder

Microphones
2 x Sennheiser MD.816T 'shotgun' condenser location mics
2 x Shure SM.89 'shotgun' condenser location mics
1 x Shure VP.88 single point MS. stereo condenser microphone
1 x Sony ECM.909A stereo microphone

Field recording equipment
1 x Shure FP.32 A 'E.N.G' portable stereo mixer
1 x pair Sony CD.550 stereo headphones
3 x 'Rycote' Zeppelin windshields
3 x 'Rycote' windjammers
Cable ties, velcro, high density foam and lots of 'gaffer' tape

Post-production & editing
1 x Allen & Heath GL.3000 mixing console
1 x Midas XL.42 stereo parametric equaliser
1 x Klark Teknik DN.6000 stereo real-time analyser
Digidesign Protools III, Apple Mac 9600/300
Digidesign Masterlist CD V.2.0

Mastering machines
Marantz CDR650
Sony DTC 1000ES DAT

The sound of these cars is a powerful ingredient in their appeal - to recreate that experience as accurately as possible, we first tried using radio mikes to limit the amount of recording equipment on board. However, we were defeated by interference from the unscreened high voltages emitted, particularly by the old cars, which made any decent recording impossible.

We then swopped to small Portadat recorders, though even they were somewhat over-sized for the single-seaters, requiring the dismantling of body panels or heroics from the driver who had to work around the machine strapped inside the cockpit. As extra protection special windshields were constructed - a wind rush of over 100 mph can drown out even a Formula 1 engine - and anti-interference boxes devised.

We recorded all the cars starting up, making a standing start, passing at speed and in-car, and then selected the most significant and impressive for the CD. The circuit diagrams below indicate the microphone positions used at Silverstone and Donington (the latter only for the BRM).

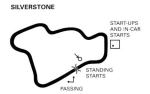

SILVERSTONE

START-UPS AND IN-CAR STARTS

STANDING STARTS

PASSING

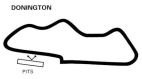

DONINGTON

PITS

A century of nose profiles shows how the racing car has become lower and wider and tyres have done much the same. The bodywork, too, has been adapted to make use of the passing airflow and provide downforce. Mechanical and aerodynamic improvement certainly, but aesthetics remain a matter for the onlooker.

ERA B Type
1936

page 44

Frazer Nash Le Mans Replica
1949

page 52

BRM V16 Mk 2
1953

page 58

Jaguar D-Type
1955

page 66

Alfa Romeo TZ
1964

page 106

Ferrari 512S
1970

page 114

Ferrari 365 GTB/4 Daytona
1972

page 122

Porsche 935 K3
1978

page 130

Ferrari F40
1989

page 166

Porsche 962
1990

page 172

McLaren F1 GTR
1995

page 180

Ferrari Enzo
2003

page 190

Panhard B1   1901

In the beginning

Ninety years is more than the average lifetime. Most things that date back this far are static, fixed, architectural. Monuments to man's creativity, but not his desire to move.

There is nothing remotely like the Panhard today, and at first it is difficult to think of this ornately leather-trimmed box as a car. You climb up via the passenger side to a ship's bridge and slide across into the leather driver's seat which curves to fit as if you had slumped into a softly padded coal scuttle. Scan the controls. Brightly plated steel levers and knobs abound everywhere, with tubes and copper pipes leading down to the engine room so the sense of ambience is more ship than car. There's no clue to what the levers might operate, but there is a steering wheel. It is absolutely horizontal, thick and wood-rimmed, sitting atop a long pole like a bird table, but it is perfectly natural to hold. The pedals are familiar too, although treading them is like squeezing a bulldog clip. You get little sense of which is clutch, brake or accelerator.

The engine starts easily at the wind of a handle and settles down to an asthmatic chugging tickover, and this transformation from stagecoach to motor car immediately imparts a greater sense of the machine's age. The five litre, four cylinder engine clanks and thumps with a complicated mixture of mechanical ferment as if its variety is some kind of aural parts count. If this was a modern engine, you'd shut it down forthwith before a connecting rod or something came crashing through the side. But no, this is perfectly normal, as is the 75 rpm tickover. So slow you can almost count the bangs as the quartet of buzzing coils fires the four big sparking plugs.

Push down the clutch, which turns out to be the one on the left. Grasp the chromed gearlever, which sits just to the right of the seat and looks like a handbrake. Lift the end of the handle to release the lock and slide the lever forward, searching for the notch which indicates first gear. It moves only forward and back, rather than across a gate, and there's no effort involved. Neither are there any clues as to how well you're doing until suddenly, there's a deep grating noise. Not horrible, but like a robotic dog growling. This grating slows to a measurable tooth count and with luck those teeth are then in mesh. Press the accelerator and the chuffing and clanking grows more frantic, but somehow it doesn't suggest the engine is turning any faster. More as if you've opened a door somewhere to let out more noise. Let the clutch up gently. The Panhard shudders, then springs forward, while a moaning noise tells you the gears are stirring in the box.

Time almost immediately for a gear change. Reach for the lever and unlock the catch. Dip the clutch, let the mechanical chuffing and puffing subside by releasing the accelerator. Gently slide the gearlever forward.

I always thought it would be fun to own a veteran car, based almost entirely on going along to the start of the London-to-Brighton with my Dad and, of course, seeing the film 'Genevieve'.

Knowing next to nothing about this kind of car, and being too idle to do any research, I had no idea what to look for. The American enthusiast Joel Finn - who has aided and abetted me in the purchase of a number of cars - made a convincing case for the Panhard, maintaining it was far superior to what he disparagingly, but accurately, called the small-engined "puddle-jumpers" and that the amount of horse-power lurking under the bonnet was "almost cheating". Big-engined cars from this era are not that common, and the great thing about the Panhard's five litre engine is that the car can tackle a steep hill even when loaded to the gunwales with friends, family and mechanics.

Importantly for me, this particular Panhard had clearly had a racing history. After its competition days were over, it had been remodelled in the 'Roi des Belges' style for its American buyer. Since manu-facturers had little interest in the body-work, this was usually left to the individual

taste of the owner, who in this case seems to have been influenced by a visit to Harrods' furniture department. He then took the car on a grand tour of Europe: the power of the engine must have made it a good tourer, although personally I wouldn't fancy tackling the downhill sections of alpine passes with the rather primitive brakes. A leisurely spin round the Netherlands would be fine.

It is sometimes difficult to remind yourself that this car was enormously advanced for its time, with a proper clutch, and a steering wheel - a real leap forward given some of the terrifying steering mechanisms of the period. By modern standards the engineering is crude, but it was simple enough for the driver, his chauffeur and - in the absence of any garages - a local blacksmith to mend at the side of the road. We've been known to continue this tradition by carrying out a repair on the valve gear with nothing more than a hammer and an old wire coathanger.

The Panhard has taken part in two dozen Brighton runs, and is usually an early finisher, failing only once when a tyre burst. We had no spare and the local tyre and exhaust centre was unable to oblige.

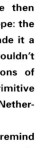

You think you have second, but no. The engine speeds up again as you release clutch and tread accelerator, and the car slowly coasts to a halt. Soon you realise that the gears have to be fished for all the time. You need to wait for a subtly different grating that says a higher gear is meshing with its mate. It's a procedure that rewards patience and a little slide of the lever back and forth to check for the catch which tells you the lever has found a slot. Then up with the clutch and the car leaps forward once more. Then again as you find third. It's as if the car slows the engine rather than the engine accelerates the car, but there's no doubt that everything is gathering speed and by now the whole platform is alive. The bridge in front is gently shaking and shuddering and you realise that you are travelling at 30, maybe even 40 mph.

Somehow you'd imagine it would be slower and more difficult, but after a little practice it's not. I had just been concentrating so much on finding the gear that I had hardly noticed the steering. Move the wheel - or try to - and at first you'd think that the mechanism had seized. That the tyres were flat. Nothing moves, the wooden rim of the wheel feels solid, immovable. But again it's not. Square up to it, tuck the elbows in to brace the shoulders and keep trying. As if by chance the Panhard will suddenly dart right, or left and you realise that it responds to pressure rather than movement. One lock to the other is less than a quarter of a turn in total and what I initially thought was mechanical malady is actually a steering mechanism with no rack or steering box to gear down the effort and allow you to wind the wheel. It's completely direct, like steering a monster kart.

By now the Panhard is chugging along quite happily, gears groaning and moaning their musical accompaniment. I discover a fourth gear in the selection which is so high that almost every bang from each one and a bit litre cylinder imparts its own individual shake to

the structure. I also find that simply flooring the accelerator is not necessarily the way to maximum engine power. You have to experiment with different amounts until the chugging up front becomes more regular, suggesting that more cylinders are firing more often. In defence against any newly discovered speed, I lean forward against the icy breeze while the camera car alongside with its collection of incredulous faces indicates between 40 and 50mph.

I suspect I was, like most people, guilty of assuming the run was mainly an excuse for dressing up, but experience has taught me that considerable skill is required to keep these brutes going in a straight line, let alone coaxing the gearbox into surrendering another gear. Entering Madeira Drive in Brighton gives you as great a sense of satisfaction as a chequered flag.

Fortunately, I had been forewarned about the brakes and decide to try them well before Stowe Corner which is looming. Just as well, because nothing whatever happens when I press the pedal. They only operate on the back wheels anyway and there's no telling whether this is as good as they get, or whether something is wrong. The sensation is something I would experience on most of the pre-war cars so Stowe would have to come and we would have to go round it, but remarkably, there's no drama. Screw the wheel to the right as if I'm giving a final nip to the lock on some vintage boiler flue, lean the body to be ready for whatever, and... round it goes. Next corner I won't bother with the brakes, then.

It's just a shame that the most important event for veteran cars is held in November. The Panhard's picnic hampers seem rather extraneous on a bitterly cold morning when the windchill factor makes you extremely glad you're wearing those funny goggles and half a hundredweight of animal pelts.

Looking at the huge stagecoach-sized wheels, each wearing a tyre barely wider than a pedal cycle's, it's hard to believe the Panhard corners as well as it does. There is however no real clue as to how its limit - whatever that may be - will announce itself. When it came it was with a giant wobble of steering and bonnet which shimmied its way back through the whole car like a farm tractor driven too fast. The bridge ahead went one way, the bonnet another, while the front tyres hopped and juddered across the road.

This was turn-of-the-century understeer and yet it didn't feel dangerous. I never felt that the Panhard might fall over. True, it was riding on Silverstone's super-smooth surface rather than the rutted roads of the early 1900s, but the Panhard's simple chassis was altogether more drivable than I had ever expected. Ninety years old, but clearly way ahead of its time.

René Panhard and his partner Emile Levassor's pioneering marque found success in the very early days of motor racing as joint winners, with Peugeot, of the first ever road trial in 1894, and six years later as outright winners of the Gordon Bennett Cup, the precursor of the modern Grand Prix series.

This car, chassis number 2649, is probably the only survivor of the handful of the B1 models originally built. It was slightly modified for racing, with a number of additional features, including a 20% overdrive on fourth gear, an extra-large water-cooling tank and a special four-branch exhaust system. The car was entered in the 1901 Paris-Nice race, which it won with Léonce Girardot at the wheel. After the race it was re-bodied with a rear door and bought by the New Yorker Willis Kilmon for a six-month grand tour of Europe; he later sold it to the opera singer James Melton.

Panhard B1

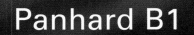

Specification

Engine capacity / configuration	5114 cc / 4 cylinders in line
Valve gear	Automatic atmospheric inlet valves, camshaft-operated side exhaust valves
Power	50 bhp @ 1400 rpm
Power to weight ratio	37 bhp per ton
Transmission	Rear drive, 4 speed and reverse, chain final drive
Tyre sizes	Front: 875 x 105 / Rear: 895 x 135
Wheelbase	2300 mm (7 ft 6.5 ins)
Track	1370 mm (4 ft 6 ins) / Rear: 1420 mm (4 ft 8 ins)
Brakes	Rear only: foot-operated contracting band; transmission handbrake
Length	3580 mm (11 ft 9 ins)
Width	1680 mm (5 ft 6 ins)
Height	1600 mm (5 ft 3 ins)
Weight	1102 kg (2424 lbs)
Front suspension	Beam axle, semi-elliptic springs
Rear suspension	Beam axle, semi-elliptic springs
Top Speed	60 mph approx.
0-40 mph	36.4 seconds

Bugatti T35B   1927

Art meets engineering

F

orget the history for a moment and just look at the elegant blue tapered body. The engine-turned dash. The spoked wheels on sculptured suspension. The horseshoe grille which has been a motif for the marque for ever.

It is an elegance, though, which is more than skin deep. Under the elaborately ventilated bonnet lies a tall, shining, rectangular engine, for all the world hewn from a solid block of metal and looking like some artistic mock-up, filling the space until the real nuts and bolts item arrives from the factory. It is obvious that such things mattered greatly to Ettore Bugatti, who was born in Italy, but lived in France all his life. No engineering expediency was allowed to compromise the appearance of his Type 35. Never mind the style of the time, a Bugatti Type 35 still looks perfectly formed seven decades later.

Admiring the car from a distance is a great pleasure. Driving it, though, might just spoil the illusion. I am fully aware how successful the car has been and I know what a wonderful noise it makes, but I also know how old it is. When it first rolled from the Bugatti factory near Strasbourg, things we take for granted like the refrigerator and the jet engine were still to be invented. And yet the Type 35 is not short of power. That supercharged straight eight work of art devours methyl alcohol and turns it into 160 horsepower. Enough, as it turned out, to accelerate the car to 60mph in less than six seconds. Going fast on the straight is one thing, though, cornering is another, and the Type 35 is equipped with tyres half the width of a modern motorcycle's and no shock absorbers to speak of. It is also extremely narrow across the axles because this was the technology of the time.

There is a starting ritual which needs to be followed precisely. Turn on the fuel tap, then pump the wooden handle on the dash to pressurise the fuel tank and feed alcohol to the carburettor. Then retard the magneto by sliding a lever in the dash, flick the ignition switch on and get someone to crank the starting handle. One heave and the engine gently burbles into action. Pressurise the tank again, advance the ignition and prepare to wrestle with the gears.

The clutch pedal is cramped against the tunnel, so you have to point the toe rather than tread the foot, but its action is so very light thanks to a part-centrifugal action which also means that too many revs will make it grab. Whatever you do, pulling the chromed gearlever across towards the cockpit and back into the slot for first is the subject of much grating and gnashing. There seems to be no way to do this nicely, so you just try and surprise the whirring teeth and get it over with.

The first thing that struck me, aged seven, about these cars was the wonderful engine-turned dashboard and the way the cockpit felt like a submarine with its brass taps, pipes and levers. For anyone who is irresistibly drawn to mechanical objects, the exquisite detail of Bugatti's engineering is completely mesmerising.

With so many victories to its name, Bugatti was an obvious target when I started thinking about buying an old racing car, and turned out to be the only good investment recommended by a financial adviser whose other suggestions ultimately led him to spend some time at Her Majesty's pleasure. We were discussing the 35B and he mentioned he knew someone who needed to sell off this particular car.

I was introduced to Richard l'Anson of Tula Engineering, who was in charge of restoring the car. He led me to the bottom of his garden, proudly pointing out a ramshackle chicken-shed, and was then forced to direct my attention a little more closely to the rusty frame leaning against it. It was not immediately obvious to me that this

A racing start then requires you to hold the handbrake next the gear lever with the right hand to stop the clutch creeping the car forward while you build the revs. Floor the throttle, drop the left foot from the pedal and at the same time transfer the right hand to the gearlever. If you don't, there's a grating shriek and the lever will flick itself back to neutral - just to spite you. If not, the surge forward is surprising, and only afterwards do you see that just the one rear wheel has laid a black line on the road. The engine's eight cylinder hum has meanwhile turned to a crackle and in no time it's time for second gear.

The gate is an upside-down mirror of a modern shift, so you keep the lever to the left and push it straight forward - which is easier to say than do. If you give the clutch pedal a brief prod just as you slide the lever then it might slip seamlessly into second. A pause gives the clutch mechanism a chance to engage and then the lever simply will not move. No grating or gnashing, just no gear. The only course of action then is to go back to first and start again, by which time the rest of the field will have disappeared. For some reason third seems easier, back and to the right, and fourth easier still. You can almost do this in one fluid movement without touching the clutch.

was a must-have item, but the silver-tongued Richard's description of what it would eventually look like convinced me that within 18 months I would be nonchalantly climbing into a gleaming Bugatti.

It was five years - and several increases in Tula's hourly rates - later that the 35B was wheeled out, but I have to admit the wait was worth it. Michael Whiting carried out much of the work at Tula, and it is a tribute to his painstakingly high standards that the car has been competing for 20 years and has probably been the most reliable of all my racing cars, despite the notorious reputation Bugattis have for being complicated and temperamental.

The gears dominate the Bugatti driving experience at first, but a little practice teaches you not to give the engine a great rev up on the change down and makes you rest a foot on the clutch rather than pushing it straight to the floor. And like riding a bike, soon you wonder where the problem was. Clean shifts become more and more a feature of the lap, each still to be savoured rather than taken for granted. Then, once you have mastered this simple task and avoided the embarrassment of coasting through a corner, trying to hold yourself in the seat, steering with one hand and fumbling for gears with the other, you can begin to understand the chassis.

Try not to grip too tight on the big wooden rim which covers those lovely carved spokes in front of you. Let the car dart this way and that - something it does without apparently moving off line - and build up speed. Then it wil be time to tackle the brakes. At first, the Bugatti driving process has a tendency to dissect itself into a series of separate actions. The trick to smooth progress is to unite them. Meanwhile the middle pedal is solid. There's nothing at all. At first you'd swear there's a block of wood under your foot because nothing, absolutely nothing is happening. For a moment, the driver's worst nightmare flashes through the mind. Is there something wrong with the brakes or is this the state of 1920s frictional art?

Then you realise that the car is beginning to shed speed. The huge finned drums inside the spoked wheels are operated by cables and chains and because operation is purely mechanical, the brakes are either on or off with little sense of quantity in between. A lap or two later had me more used to them and with familiarity came carelessness. On the next lap, going towards Stowe Corner, I trod the pedal much harder, but instead of locking a wheel, the mechanical compensation which Bugatti used to balance the system from side to side kicked in and the car dived towards the edge of the track. I dared not release pressure on the pedal because I wouldn't then make the corner. My fingers curled ever more firmly round that rim as I tried to counter the swerve, only for the Type 35 to leap the opposite way. Then it did the whole thing over again. Thankfully, the leap this time was smaller, and then smaller still, until I scrabbled round the corner. It is just something you learn not to do, and a limit that arrives in a way you don't expect. This really should have prepared me for a trip over the kerbs.

The Paddock chicane on Silverstone's South circuit is intended for modern cars. Their suspension can float over smooth kerbing with just enough disturbance to let the driver know that this is the edge of the track. My Bugatti confidence was growing, gears slipping in with increasing facility and my body which had hitherto felt

There is an assumption that components for such elderly and rare cars are hard to find, but an extraordinary network exists of restorers, engineers and car clubs - and since the parts were handmade then, they can be handmade now. It takes time, but at least you don't need a fully equipped factory.

This recycling of parts can, however, lead to embarrassingly tight-lipped scenes in the paddock as more than one historic car appears to have the same identity and chassis number. But these occasional contretemps are probably preferable to the obsessiveness of the infamous Schlumpf brothers, who stockpiled parts for their collection of 400-odd cars, often moving both cars and parts into their museum in Mulhouse under cover of darkness. The museum, seized by the French government in lieu of tax, contains one exhibit which typifies their crazed worship in a bizarre tableau featuring a full-sized racing Bugatti flanked by two miniature Type 52s and overlooked by a picture of the brothers' mother.

The 35B is a pure racing car. Road use is not generally recommended: the car runs on methyl alcohol (not normally available at your local service station), only does three miles to the gallon if pushed hard, and the plugs have to be changed according to the kind of driving you are planning. It is also unspeakably noisy, traumatising cows and sheep in its wake, as I once found out when severely reprimanded by an apoplectic farmer - I had foolishly stopped, mistaking his gesticulations for the sign of an enthusiast.

Having, as so often happens, never had a test drive in the car, I was taken aback by its unbelievably heavy handling. I thought this was what real men drove, until I invited a Bugatti expert, Hamish Moffat, to try the car round the old Nürburgring. "My God," he said upon returning, "You're a hero." The axle wedges had been fitted upside down, requiring me to exert enormous extra pressure on the steering wheel. It just proves that even the most talented expert probably only knows 95% of any vintage car's intricacies...

so exposed, was beginning to sink down and move about the Bugatti's cockpit. Leaning forward against the cornering force freed the arms and shoulders to feel the sensitivity of the steering. I was learning the technique of easing the car oh so gently towards the apex, squeezing on the power, then waiting for the little surge of revs which told me the inside rear wheel was lifting from the road. I would just back off a touch and unravel a degree or two of lock to recover the lost momentum and try not to provoke the car again. If I did, another little wheel-sawing ritual restored equilibrium. The lap times were coming down nicely.

I learnt that turning late and sharp simply upset the bendy chassis and had the inside rear wheel way off the ground, spinning impotently, but turning early let me keep the power on for longer. Confidence tempted me to take a modern line across the kerbs at the chicane. What happened then was a timely reminder of how brave were the men who drove these cars on the roads of the 1920s, roads where all the surface was like Silverstone chicane kerbing. The Bugatti's front right wheel rode the first hump, followed by the rear. The T35 arched and bobbed like a boat over a wave, yawing to the left. Then came the opposite kerb, and this seemed to catch the Bugatti in mid leap, twitching the car into a violent series of pogo hops, bouncing from one front wheel to the opposite rear and back again. A bit like the dance under braking, but along its length rather than across its beam and a motion which kicked the driver's rump from its perch with yet greater force. But, like the braking episode, the hopping seemed to have a natural cycle, after which it faded away like a spinning coin settling on a table. Maybe they got used to such things in the 1920s. Maybe they fought it and paid the price for bravery.

You could twitch and slide the Bugatti for ever, and as long as you stayed away from bumps and treated the brakes with respect, the 35 was a very honest racer. Its steering was much sharper and nicer to use than many of the cars which came after and once you learnt to let the car flow at its own pace rather than to force it, the Bugatti was fast too. Much faster than I expected and quicker than a great many more modern cars.

I will remember for a long time the noise of that square and shining engine. Not to me the ripping fabric of legend, but more the strident hum of a French horn with just the hint of a rasp at the edge. Art meets engineering. An unforgettable piece of history.

The Type 35 was built between 1924 and 1931 at the company's Molsheim works in Alsace. Following the initial impressive success of the factory-entered cars in major competitions throughout Europe, Bugatti produced cars in sufficient quantities for privateers to race. The T35B was the supercharged development of the original normally aspirated version, and of the 360-odd built nearly half remain.

Little is known about the history of this particular car - the frame number 369 giving an original construction date of 1927. After Hamish Moffat brought the complete rolling chassis to England in the 1950s, intermittent rebuilding continued until Tula Engineering finished the restoration work in time for the 1978 racing season. That year the car won its class at the Nürburgring Historic Meeting, and has been competing ever since. Now designated chassis BOC 007, it is regarded as one of the fastest Type 35Bs in existence.

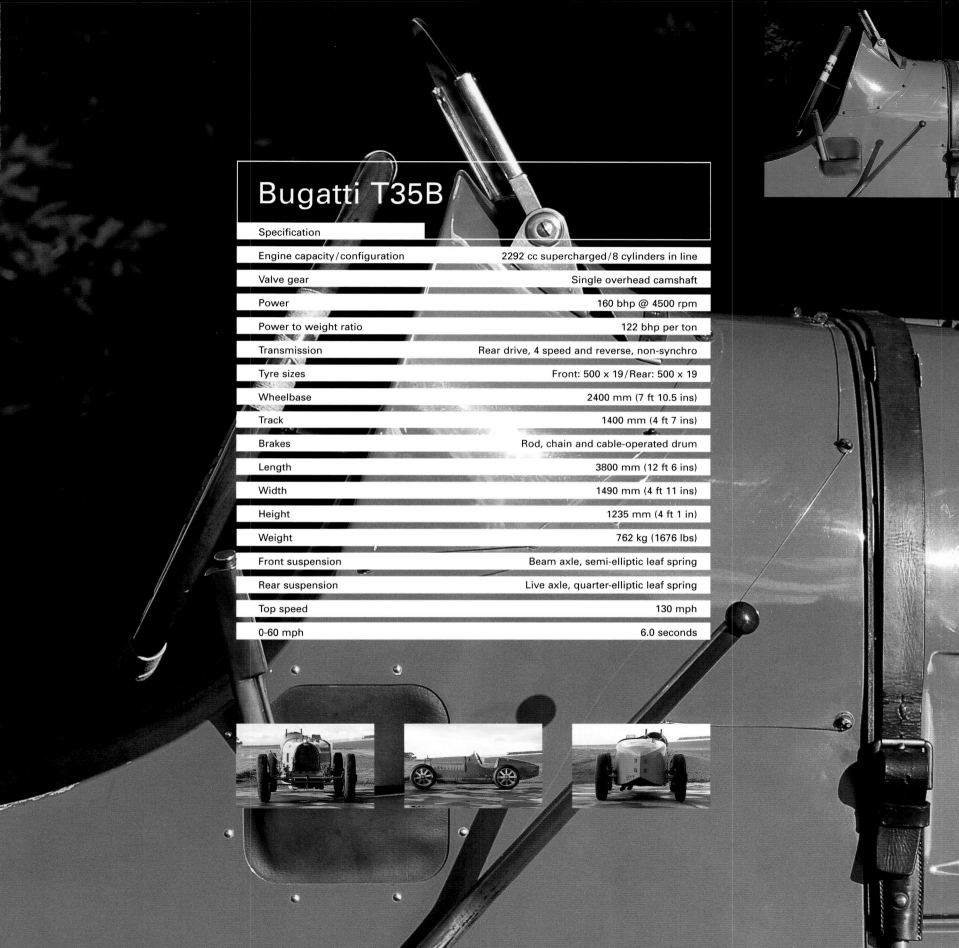

Bugatti T35B

Specification

Engine capacity / configuration	2292 cc supercharged / 8 cylinders in line
Valve gear	Single overhead camshaft
Power	160 bhp @ 4500 rpm
Power to weight ratio	122 bhp per ton
Transmission	Rear drive, 4 speed and reverse, non-synchro
Tyre sizes	Front: 500 x 19 / Rear: 500 x 19
Wheelbase	2400 mm (7 ft 10.5 ins)
Track	1400 mm (4 ft 7 ins)
Brakes	Rod, chain and cable-operated drum
Length	3800 mm (12 ft 6 ins)
Width	1490 mm (4 ft 11 ins)
Height	1235 mm (4 ft 1 in)
Weight	762 kg (1676 lbs)
Front suspension	Beam axle, semi-elliptic leaf spring
Rear suspension	Live axle, quarter-elliptic leaf spring
Top speed	130 mph
0-60 mph	6.0 seconds

Alfa Romeo 8C 2300   1931

Class of eight

Alfa Romeo 8C 2300

The Alfa 8 cylinder bonnet is very long and very louvred. It needs to be because the engine beneath it measures 38 5/8 inches.

A fluted, curved, rounded piece of the foundryman's art with eight boreholes. A sculpture in aluminium that looks like chromium-plated marble, picked out with little inspection covers, each held with chromed and domed fasteners. The sort of thing accountants would replace with pieces of pressed tin. And nestling alongside this piece of automotive expression is another anachronism. A supercharger, driven by a shaft and gears rather than any piece of rubber belt. An aluminium pump, scalloped and polished to match the engine and to feed those eight cylinders with more petrol than they can suck for themselves. Feeding that diet of fuel and air not through a plastic pipe linked by rubber hoses, but by a specially cast tunnel whose fins lie in perfect symmetry with those on the engine behind it. And all this for just 2.3 litres. Art in engine building was obviously not exclusive to Bugatti.

At first, the noise from this gleaming mass of metal is a disappointment. Folklore still says eight straight cylinders make a noise like ripping fabric, but not this Alfa. It's more of a boom than a rip. Push in the ignition key to switch on the electrics and illuminate the starter button. The electric motor whirrs the eight pistons past compression with barely a stutter and the Alfa gently comes alive, moaning and chuffing as a thousand pieces of metal bump and grind before bathing themselves in a fresh coating of lubricant. And then, as you wait to warm the oil, there's more to be had by listening carefully, just as with any good piece of music. You can hear the boom become the bass, and now there's a gentle wail from the supercharger which swells as you rev up, disappears when you lift off. Just beneath that there's another, more musical warble from the exhaust. Not the demented pigeon noise of a modern five cylinder Audi, but a more orchestrated, subtler kind of rhythm, like a string bass shimmering in the background. If the little chrome-rimmed rev counter with its flickering needle were to fail, it would be this rhythm which would say how fast the engine was turning. Otherwise the hum of eight straight cylinders is so seamlessly subtle that you could hardly tell.

Seats are shiny, slippery leather. Beautifully cracked and polished by a handful of privileged backsides. Wheel is big and the rim is metal. Floor boards are wood. Pedals sprout up and back and the accelerator is in the centre, brake to the right. Why did they do that...?

I ended up paying more for this car than any other. Generally I have managed to find myself marginally ahead of the game, but in this instance I prevaricated for far too long - like about 20 years. For that entire time I kept thinking about these cars with some odd notion that prices would drop, or that one would turn up forgotten in some barn or other. Needless to say, values continued to rise and barns remain undiscovered.

My respect for this style of Alfa had developed when I'd bought a 6C some years earlier, but the end of a tour provided the opportunity of upgrading to an 8C. Within minutes, it seemed, the dealers had picked up the scent and for a period I felt immense empathy for a fox on the run. Finally I decided that I would opt for the car which offered the best history, succumbing to the argument that I might be paying twice the money but I would be getting three times the car.

The history included the fact that this car had been driven by Enzo Ferrari in his last-ever race. He finished second, losing to

Alfa Romeo 8C 2300

But I must make sure I remember. This car has cost more than any other of these cars. Door is low and tiny, shuts with a minimal clunk. So low that my elbow won't even rest on the ledge. Line of sight is over the top or round to the right of the ornately framed screen. I feel comfortable and that length of bonnet is a reassuring amount of metal up ahead. And yet I can't help a feeling of sitting on the Alfa rather than in it.

Moving off adds yet more to the soundtrack. The gears screech and shriek their protest at the passing of half a century and more, a harsh sound which all but blots out the symphony from under the bonnet. The gearlever stretches up and back like a curved wand, sprouting from a dinky little chrome-plated gate atop the gearbox. Flop the lever about the neutral groove and it feels so light and easy that the gearbox might be missing. Move it left and forward to the first of the two forward gates and feel the grind of every tooth as the gears engage. There's no effort, but as with the Bugatti, you just cannot hurry. If the grating offends, the only way is to wait an age for the gears to stop stirring.

Once you're on the move, the chassis feels immediately more accommodating than the gearbox and the brakes are good despite their cable operation - vastly better than the Bugatti's which look similar in size. Remember that the brake pedal is the one on the right, and to squeeze it rather than push it hard - everything must be done gently for fear of triggering another warping contest between axles, primitive friction shock absorbers and flexible chassis rails. Not that this is in any

a smaller 6C Alfa, but there was no shame in this: I would have thought it an honour to be overtaken by arguably one of the greatest drivers of all time, Tazio Nuvolari. As the Commendatore must have discovered, the 8C looks wonderful and is a delight to drive. The engine produces power all the way through the rev band, allowing you to leave the car in fourth gear and cruise easily, but you still have the wonderful gearbox available if you're feeling more competitive.

With its sophisticated styling and engineering the Alfa 8C is often thought of as a pre-war Ferrari GTO. This particular

way downmarket, quite the reverse. Be smooth and the Alfa's variety of movement feels so organised as to be there by design. Ease the Alfa gently into the bend and you will experience the real meaning of the four-wheel drift. Hear the rear tyres whimpering in muted protest as the car's back end, complete with its pair of spare wheels, gently sways away from the corner. Use that gentle, almost imperceptible drift to start the turn, helping it along with the big metal wheel. Pour on the power to increase the yaw and hold it. Just take off a little of the lock but keep steering until the inside rear wheel starts to loosen its grip, then reapply a touch more when the Alfa wants to straighten up again.

It's easy to do, and although it is a similar process to that needed for the Bugatti, it is much less energetic and the car's responses so much more gentle. Added to which you really can hold a delicious drift in the classic style with hardly a twitch of the steering wheel. But while you may be motionless, the Alfa is certainly not. All the time you can feel the car rearranging itself. The dash moves one way, the seat moves another. The bonnet, with its mass of complex chromed catches, shimmies behind the radiator as the floor gently quakes beneath your feet. The long sweeping mudguards flap up and down like the wings of a bird gently shedding water. Every part has its own direction and the whole experience is more animal than mechanical.

style of bodywork has a touch more room than other pure racing versions, with a hood and sidescreens, so that although you can't take many friends along, you can fit in a picnic hamper and shelter from the rain. 8C Monza drivers have to go hungry and wet.

My first outing in the car was a tour of South-West Ireland over some less than perfect roads. Anything loose promptly dropped off, and a twinge of anxiety ran through me as I imagined I'd left a trail of parts strewn across County Cork, doubtless allowing some ruthless dealer to construct an identikit car from the bits, then flog it to retire into tax exile.

Like the Bugatti the Alfa inspires great devotion amongst enthusiasts, and there's a deep pool of knowledge to draw on among people who have been racing and restoring Alfas for 30 or 40 years. Not only do they know exactly which sidelight fitting is required but many of them have spent years researching the precise shade of paint used on a car of the period. Some might consider this pure folly, though without their dedication cars like these would by now have deteriorated beyond repair.

I was a late developer as an Alfa Romeo enthusiast, but when the lady selling me the 6C handed over its documentation she showed me a photograph of her late husband racing the car. The photo revealed the Alfa with a vintage Bentley in hot pursuit. I recognised the Bentley instantly: it was my father racing at Silverstone. Any car that could manage to hold off my Dad had to be good. That was it - I saw the light immediately.

The Alfa then reminds you of its 1930s technology in simple but memorable fashion. Either the driver's door pops open in mid-corner, or the shiny leather seat gives up on your overalls and you slide helplessly towards the passenger space. Anticipate these, brace yourself and prepare to push the 8C beyond its will and all four wheels will slide wide, leading neither with front end or back. Use too much of its supercharged power in an attempt to extend the drift without carrying enough speed and the inside rear wheel will spin it all away. None of this is at all dramatic.

Because the 8C doesn't immediately announce its limits in dramatic and unstable fashion, it is all too easy to forget its 66-year vintage. Soothe it along rather than try and hurry it, wait for the gears rather than risk a crunch, use the wheel sparingly and the inertia with care and it proves to be a really classy machine.

Designed by Vittorio Jano, the Alfa Romeo 8C was in production for only four years. This early car - chassis number 2111007 - was first registered to Scuderia Ferrari and was one of two cars entered by the Scuderia for the Targa Florio of May 1931. It was driven by Luigi Arcangeli, but he was substituted by Freddy Zehender after being injured by a flying stone.

The car was also driven by Enzo Ferrari in his last ever race, when he finished second to Tazio Nuvolari in the 1931 Circuito delle Tre Provincie (picture above). Sold on by Ferrari after taking part in that year's Coppa della Consuma hill-climb, when Baconin Borzacchini finished second to Nuvolari, the car competed in the 1932 Mille Miglia and placed fifth. Over the past 80 years the Alfa has been used constantly, the previous owner having run it regularly over Irish roads for 30-odd years, as well as taking part in occasional competitions.

Alfa Romeo 8C 2300

Specification	
Engine capacity/configuration	2336 cc supercharged/8 cylinders in line
Valve gear	Twin overhead camshafts
Power	155 bhp @ 5200 rpm
Power to weight ratio	156 bhp per ton
Transmission	Rear drive, 4 speed and reverse, non-synchro
Tyre sizes	Front: 500 x 19/Rear: 600 x 19
Wheelbase	2750 mm (9 ft 0 ins)
Track	1380 mm front and rear (4 ft 6 ins)
Brakes	Rod-operated drums
Length	4200 mm (13 ft 9 ins)
Width	1500 mm (4 ft 11 ins)
Height	1270 mm (4 ft 2 ins)
Weight	1027 kg (2259 lbs)
Front suspension	Beam axle, semi-elliptic leaf springs
Rear suspension	Live axle, semi-elliptic leaf springs
Top speed	120 mph
0-60 mph	9.4 seconds

Aston Martin Ulster   1935

Honest Englishman

This is the car that turned Mason the musician into Mason the racer, and besides affection for a very English make, it's easy to see why. The Ulster is not as handsome as the French or Italian cars but instead looks simple and friendly.

The axles stick out either side of the body, bolted to simple cart springs, so there's no tricky suspension to corrupt the handling. The engine, too, should be easy to live with - it has only four cylinders, a pair of carburettors and no supercharger. Lift the bonnet and there lies a simple rectangular block of cast iron, topped with an aluminium cover. No fins, no flutes, no chrome, no polished sheen, nothing as imposing as the Bugatti's underbonnet, but pleasing in its very simplicity.

The gearbox is equally ordinary-looking and its aluminium case, complete with short straight gearlever and squashy rubber gearknob, is all visible from inside the cockpit. The steering wheel, by comparison, looks needlessly large and strong for the task of

As soon as I got my provisional driving licence I began learning on a 1927 Austin Seven 'Chummy', as well as trying to master the art of car maintenance. This was less successful, and by the time I swopped the 'Chummy' for the optimistically named Austin Seven 'Nippy', the only skills I seemed to have acquired were the application of Araldite and Radweld.

steering such a simple thing - why, even a working tractor of the same period would boast a smaller one. The Aston's has a thick black bakelite rim and four hefty spokes, while the dash behind it contains the bare minimum of dials. It's almost as if everything that is normally hidden is offered for display as proof of the car's straightforward nature.

Having said that, there are a couple of important things to remember. The accelerator is in the middle like the Alfa's, but the gearshift gate is also back to front. First is where we normally expect third to be, back for second, then across and left for third. All this is fine when you sit in the pits and think about it, but it's when instinct takes over as you try to be last of the late brakers before Stowe Corner that you find the problems.

The body is long and low, but the seat is high. There's no door and you have to manoeuvre your legs over the body's side, splay them to pass under the wheel and then slide them down into the tunnel. It helps if you have ball-jointed knees but those of us with mere hinges in our limbs succeed in a fair impression of a geriatric, trying to support the body while you climb in and stop the knees hitting the dash as you thread them under that huge tiller. Once there, it's comfortable enough, but as with the Alfa there's a feeling of exposure, of sitting on rather than in the car with most of your body sticking out and unprotected in the breeze. Added to which, for those of us reared on more modern machinery, you can't help noticing the lack of any belts or any rollover protection. The Aston is no different to any of Nick's other pre-war cars, but for some reason I thought about it more.

Flick the separate switches for the magneto and tick-ticking fuel pumps, retard the ignition with the steering wheel-mounted lever and hit the switch for the asthmatic-sounding starter. There's a warbly booming noise as if the sound has to reverberate all the way down the long side-mounted pipe, followed by a flatulent crackle as it escapes into the atmosphere. Press the pedal in the middle and the engine seems to take an age to build up speed and even longer to spin down, while there's a real sense of mechanical vintage about the thrumming that ripples through the Aston's frame. You can almost sense the length of crankshaft throw and sinewy connecting rod and the distance the piston has to flash up and down the cylinder bore. You feel all this through the clutch pedal which is closer to the crank than most - but it's easy to push. Just remember it's the one on the left.

The back-to-front gearlever is much closer to hand and the lever much shorter than any so far, but the gears turn out to be just as crunchy. You have to wait patiently for those revs to die away, then gently ease the lever into the next slot. That patience will be rewarded by a smooth, silent engagement. Hurrying brings about a crash of teeth. Not the deep and aggressive kind that came from the Bugatti, or the dentist's drill variety of the Alfa, but the more gentle washboard rattle of smaller gear wheels.

I then upgraded to an Aston Martin International, which was way beyond my limited mechanical knowledge. Fortunately, one of the best known Aston experts, Derrick Edwards, had a garage close to my home. I had seen Derrick race at Silverstone, and he seemed the ideal man to turn to. However, he said he was just too busy, but suggested I come back six months later. As I'd turned up in flares and sporting a Zapata moustache, I think he wanted to establish either my enthusiasm or my credit rating.

I duly returned and found that Derrick had finally had enough of the modern motor car business: he hated all paperwork and would often smear his face with oil, lie under a convenient car and mutter "Mr Edwards isn't in" when the Inland Revenue called. In extremis he would use some headed notepaper liberated from a Swiss police station to suggest he was under arrest and so unable to help them with their enquiries.

Turning his attention back to rebuilding old cars, he began work on my Aston International and was happy for me to assist. I became extremely skilled with a sandblaster, but soon developed a reputation for stripping cars and then disappearing on tour, leaving someone else to pick up the pieces.

Derrick and I talked at length about competing, and while the International was still in pieces we decided to buy an Ulster for what seemed like a fortune of £6000 - this was LM 21 and the car I entered for my first race. I don't think I'd ever been particularly encouraged to race by my Dad, although he loved the sport. Now, as a father, I think I can understand why: although I want my children to experience the thrills, the element of risk means it's important for them to discover it for themselves, rather than feeling under an obligation to have a go.

Derrick was a excellent teacher, at a time when there were very few racing schools, and when you could get a competition licence simply by writing a cheque. He knew how to set achievable targets and could often be seen during practice sessions sedately trailing two or three new drivers behind him round the track like a protective mother hen.

The Ulster is an excellent beginner's car, with wonderful handling, terrific brakes, and slightly underpowered due to its heavy but robust chassis. But it is also a great racing car, and I still enjoy driving it now as much as I ever did.

Derrick and I went on to form Morntane Engineering, a partnership dealing solely in the sale and reconstruction of pre-war Astons. This was a rapid education in the byzantine intricacies of the garage business, the appalling behaviour of some of the customers and the even worse tricks of the trade. In the mistaken belief that we should acquire more Ulsters for stock, I found myself unable to part with any of them, ending up with three works team Ulsters - LM17, 18 and 21 (which also accounts for the fact that more than one car appears in these pictures). Given the enthusiasm my children seem to be showing, I wish I'd bought more.

It did seem odd to be thinking so earnestly about varying degrees of gearbox grating, but it was such a feature of all the older cars and the racer's instinct to get on with it was constantly wrestling with any mechanical sympathy. You could wait for an age for the gears to synchronise themselves while the stopwatch ticked away, or you could put up with the palm-numbing clash. So that is why the Aston's gearknob is made from squishy rubber.

The Aston's simple unsupercharged engine feels a little breathless after the last three, and the huge chasm between third and fourth gear ratios seems enough to bury what life the engine can muster. Time after time, I would reach the 5,000 rpm limit in third halfway through a corner and decide that a shift to top gear had to be made in the interests of keeping all those flashing internals inside the engine, only to find that the car started to slow down because it could not overcome the drag from sliding tyres. It was a bit like shifting up a gear and realising you are still climbing a hill.

Despite this, the Aston was fun to drive. It went round the lap in much the same style as the Alfa, with a sharper response from the wheel followed by a slightly lesser swaying as the tail slewed wide. There was barely enough power then to increase the slide or to spin the inside rear wheel, so the slip and slide had its own duration and when the inertia was used up, the car straightened itself. This was a prompt to turn the wheel again, but you needed to resist the temptation to sling the car into the corner in some ham-fisted attempt to compensate for horsepower. As with the other simply suspended cars, the Ulster's response was to push its nose wide, or try and climb up on the edges of both outside tyres and lose you so much speed you had to shift down a gear. Here was the trick. To judge the entry speed nicely between too much and too little and then manage it smoothly all the way through. Carefully done it was possible to get a goodly drift going.

Meanwhile the Aston shook and shimmied in authentic period fashion. Wings, bonnet, headlights, dashboard, all of them wobbled and shook, each individual dance appearing to have a motion of its own which bore no relation to the car's progress. All told, the Aston didn't have quite the fluid flowing style of the Alfa and the reason for that big wheel had by now become all too apparent. You had to make a conscious effort to put it exactly where you wanted, because it was mechanically stiff and had no self-centring spring or feel to it at all. I even had to work at keeping the car straight.

The Aston was one of the few cars other than the Panhard both to sound and feel its age. This however was far from a minus point. Its simplicity and straightforward handling gave it an easy charm and it was just the sort of car you might take out for a few laps when you wanted to play without frightening yourself. Which is exactly why Nick bought it in the first place.

Aston Martin Ulster

Specification

Engine capacity/configuration	1495 cc/4 cylinders in line
Valve gear	Single overhead camshaft
Power	85 bhp @ 5000 rpm
Power to weight ratio	86 bhp per ton
Transmission	Rear drive, 4 speed and reverse, non-synchro
Tyre sizes	550 x 18 front and rear
Wheelbase	2603 mm (8 ft 6.5 ins)
Track	1435 mm (4 ft 8.5 ins)
Brakes	Cable-operated drum
Length	3987 mm (13 ft 1 in)
Width	1600 mm (5 ft 3 ins)
Height	1168 mm (8 ft 1 in)
Weight	1040 kg (2288 lbs)
Front suspension	Beam axle, semi-elliptic springs
Rear suspension	Live axle, semi-elliptic springs
Top speed	102 mph
0-60 mph	13.8 seconds

ERA B Type   1936

Thirst for alcohol

All the cars that Nick owns have their own sound. Each is memorable and an important part of the variety which distinguishes one from another. There are two, however, which stand out from the rest.

Both of them have engines which displace a mere one and a half litres and each is force-fed by an engine-driven supercharger. Both have a prodigious appetite for alcohol. The first is the BRM V16 of 1952, a legend as much for its impossible, brave complexity and its innovative engineering as its other-worldly shriek. The second is the ERA.

The ERA makes a noise like a bass saxophone and cello in duet. The strings are the tremulous whine of the supercharger that feeds the one and a half litre six cylinder engine and the sax is the rich, reedy, deep-throated, metallic sound of the exhaust. When the engine is driving hard, the clamour gargles from deep within the engine's chest, then vibrates down the long metal pipe that runs just below the cockpit side before blasting out like a freshly lit firework. When you lift off the accelerator, there's a muted crackle like a thousand ball bearings cascading over a wooden floor while the underlying bassy boom dies away with the fading engine revs. The disparate layers of sound seem to come from opposite ends of the car like two speakers at each end of a room. Walk round it and you hear different amounts of each. A supercharged methanol-fuelled exhaust note is deeper and richer than anything you will hear today and although the concert is nothing like as loud as the BRM's, it is still noisier than one and a half litres has any right to be. It brings a smile to the lips.

There are many other memorable things about the ERA. After the Bugatti of the late 1920s with its narrow, cramped cockpit and tricky gearshift, I had expected the ERA to be much the same, but the English car is as easy to operate as the French one is difficult. The ERA's seat is like something from a gentleman's club, deep and extensively padded and complete with arms on each side, covered in fading black leather which has cracked and worn with the passage of time and the energy of a multitude of drivers. Your legs bend comfortably forward and down and your feet splay to the very edges of the cockpit, resting on pedals each side of a humped, polished aluminium gearbox casing which takes up nearly the whole width of the floor. The big four-spoked steering wheel with its rope-bound rim is less than a foot from your chest, the all-important rev counter is large and prominent in the bare metal dash behind it. The aero-screen which could have been borrowed from a brand new Tiger Moth stretches just an inch or so above the wheel and lies barely a knuckle's width in front. But for the steering wheel you could so easily be sitting in something made by Hawker or de Havilland.

The ERA, perhaps more than any of the other cars, evokes childhood memories of Silverstone. I went to dozens of vintage race meetings with my father and I think I saw an ERA at virtually every one. These were the days when race control was carried out from a double-decker bus parked on the pit straight, and hospitality was a sausage roll served in the marquee. It was my idea of the perfect day out.

In the 1950s the ERA was too old for modern racing but was still one of the fastest cars available to VSCC entrants. I was already conscious of the individual cars, including the ex-Prince Bira car 'Remus', which would later be owned and raced by Patrick Lindsay, one of the owner-drivers whose great taste and driving ability I most aspired to emulate.

Over the years I had seen R10B competing, so I already had some knowledge of its qualities. The fact that Tula Engineering had been looking after the car meant that, although yet again I had not had the luxury of a test drive, I knew it was in good running order, ready to go and with plenty of spares. It was also wonderfully original, with all the correct numbered pieces - even the enamel on the little ERA badge was intact.

It's a relatively simple car, nothing like as complex as the Bugatti: if something goes wrong there's a fair chance of being able to strip and repair it in the paddock. It still puzzles me that an engine can be stripped and rebuilt overnight by dedicated mechanics if required for a race the next day, whereas normally it can take up to six months, with the accompanying bill.

The gearbox is complicated, but it's a proprietary brand pre-selector box with a lot in common with a number of road and racing cars, and parts are relatively easy to obtain. The only real problem is remembering whether you have pre-selected a higher or lower gear as you hurtle into a corner. Also the car has to be warmed up by having its rear wheels jacked off the ground to allow an extra oil pump in the gearbox to function. This is noisy and dangerous, but part of the fun, as the smell of methanol and Castrol R mingles to take you back 60 years to the heady days of Brooklands - a time when race wear consisted of flat cap, goggles, shirt-sleeves and tie, with a tweed jacket for inclement weather.

With this in mind my first outing was in the wet at Spa, not the ideal learning experience, but if you've trailered a car 300 miles it would be bad form to hide under the bed in the motorhome. With plenty of power and not much grip, my progress was in the style of Torvill and Dean. This feeling of being new to the car was exacerbated by competing against seasoned campaigners

On the left of the dash is a knob and a gauge. Pump the knob until the needle reads three pounds. This tells you your effort has pressurised the fuel tank behind you and will guarantee a supply of alcohol to the carburettor. Alcohol in its purest form is a much friendlier fuel than petrol - it liberates cooling water as it burns to soothe pre-war pistons during the heat of combustion and prevent detonation - explosions which could burst the engine's head. Less than three pounds and there's not enough pressure to push the fuel from tank to engine. Mechanically simple but something extra for the driver to do when not wrestling the steering wheel. Forget it, though, and the engine will splutter. The fuel tap on the outside of the cockpit is on, pressure is up, magnetos are on. Your assistant cranks the starting handle half a turn and the engine bursts into life. The notion of hand cranking a Formula 1 car takes some getting used to, but after a while it makes perfect sense...

Engine up to temperature, driver seated in the armchair and it's time to go. But before you do, there are a couple of things to be learnt. To the right and below the dash is a simple vertical up-and-down gate with a little metal lever that looks as if it was borrowed from a farm machine. This controls another of the ERA's defining characteristics, the Wilson pre-selector gearbox. When other drivers were wrestling to synchronise Bugatti or Aston gears the ERA driver had no such problems. It goes like this. Engine crackling and whining at a lumpy 1,000rpm tickover. Neutral is selected but the car creeps and jerks with every surge of revs, trying to move like a modern automatic in 'drive' at the traffic lights. Mustn't dally, the ERA chapter says that this is a bad time for the Wilson. The pumps in the gearbox are not turning to circulate the oil and the clutches will be wearing. This is why part of the essential ERA equipment is a large cantilever jack like an automotive Zimmer frame. This slips under the rear axle and lifts the rear wheels off the ground to let them spin while the engine warms.

Move the little knob out of its slot and up to the next one. This is first. Press the clutch, feel it click under your foot. Feel the car jerk as if someone has bumped the boot. Lift clutch and press accelerator and drive away normally. Now, whether you want to shift or not, move the lever up another slot. There's no effort and there's no sense of moving any machinery like shifting a manual gearbox. Then, just dip clutch pedal up and down while lifting off the power. Your feet perform just as they would when shifting normally - your hands, though, remain firmly on the wheel.

The shift happens as if a magic hand has flicked the gearlever - like when young son moves the gearlever while dad works the pedals. But the faster you move your feet, the quicker it changes, up or down.

like Patrick Marsh, who was capable of arriving back in the paddock after the race and discussing the revs I was pulling on the straight, since he'd had time to read my rev counter as we were running abreast.

This is another make that generates intense loyalty and has one of the better owners' clubs. Since there were little more than 20 ERAs produced, and only 13 B types, you'd think it would be one of the most exclusive, but this is not the case. You don't have to own an ERA: the only membership requirement is a shared enthusiasm for the cars (and a crisp fiver).

You can be in top gear flat out down the straight at Silverstone and after you have pumped the knob to boost the alcohol pressure, you can just gently move the gear selector to third. There will be no immediate response and nothing at all will happen until you dip the clutch ready for the corner. The ease of control that the Wilson brings, in an age before synchromesh and low inertia gearboxes were even thought of, is delightful, and yet there were many who could not get on with it and some ERAs were converted to a more conventional gnash and crash type of shift.

Out on the circuit, the next surprise is the brakes. Where the Bugatti seemed hardly to slow at all, the ERA's pedal has real bite and under normal braking the car tracks straight and true. Tread too hard, though, and the wheels don't so much lock, as tramp viciously, setting off a waving, snaking shudder through the entire chassis. The whole car feels totally out of control when this happens so it is best avoided, but it does give some clue as to the flexible nature of a simple ladder frame chassis.

Squeeze the brakes before the long right hander after the South circuit's pits. Feel them bite with just the one skip of the tyres telling you that judder was close. Kick the clutch and tap the accelerator. Third gear slips in perfectly with no effort at all. Ease the big wheel to the right to get that bendy chassis tweaked and ready. Without realising I will have shifted body to the left and pushed thighs and backside into the corner of the armchair. Shoulders are already hunched and arms bent. The wheelrim is less than a foot from a head bent forward. All to try and brace the body so that I don't hang on to the wheel. The car turns, then quickly slips its tail to the left. Lean the shoulders instinctively in the same direction and the wheel straightens with them. Keep the power on and hold it. The ERA drifts beautifully. Listen to the engine revs rising as the bendy chassis lifts one rear corner and unsticks a tyre. No more than 6,000 rpm now. Hope I've remembered to flick the gearlever one notch down. Listen to the blasting saxophonic sound. Time to follow the road left. Tap the clutch, feel fourth slip in. Shift bum right and shoulders left. Right elbow goes up in the air. Try not to hang on to the wheel but make sure it moves enough to steer the car. The ERA's boat tail skips to the right. Sit up straight. Tuck in right elbow to pull that big wheel just a corrective inch or so. Don't fidget with the helm, let the car do the work. Kiss the green grass with the right rear wheel. With any luck we should be straight. Time to pump the pressure knob and flick the gearknob to third, ready for Club Corner, then settle down behind the aeroscreen and take helmet out of the freezing slipstream.

It looks unreal... said one onlooker. As if it wasn't meant to travel that fast and somehow the driver is required to carry it. All those arms and elbows and crawling and scrabbling about in the cockpit they said. It looks so animated. It isn't the charade it might be, but you can't help it. It seems totally natural, necessary even, but it probably makes the driving look harder than it is, because the ERA is a very well-behaved little car. Most of the scrambling is to get the body braced so that you can work the wheel if you need to. Belts and tight fitting seats were some years off.

English Racing Automobiles launched their first car, the A Type (chassis R1A), at Brooklands in May 1934, designed for the contemporary 1500 cc voiturette formula. This was second only to Grand Prix racing in importance, and the training ground for its future stars. Chassis R10B is one of thirteen B Types first produced in 1935 and helped earn this design the reputation of being the most consistently successful 'pure' racing car Britain had ever produced.

Peter Whitehead, this car's first owner, raced it with Peter Walker internationally - Whitehead winning the Australian Grand Prix in 1938 (top picture). After the Second World War the ERAs found an extra lease of life as competition cars: this car finished seventh in the 1947 French Grand Prix, again driven by Peter Whitehead. It also competed in the first post-war British Grand Prix at Silverstone in October 1948, when Peter Walker's new E-type ERA GP1 broke a timing gear in practice and R10B was substituted for the race, finishing 11th.

ERA B Type

Specification

Engine capacity/configuration	1488 cc supercharged/6 cylinders in line
Valve gear	Twin high cams, short pushrods and rockers
Power	150 bhp @ 6500 rpm
Power to weight ratio	207 bhp per ton
Transmission	Rear drive, 4 speed and reverse pre-select
Tyre sizes	Front: 550 x 16/Rear: 650 x 16
Wheelbase	2438 mm (8 ft 0 ins)
Track	1333 mm (4 ft 4.5 ins)/Rear: 1219 mm (4 ft 0 ins)
Brakes	Rod-operated drum
Length	3556 mm (11 ft 8 ins)
Width	1574 mm (5 ft 2 ins)
Height	1168 mm (3 ft 10 ins)
Weight	738 kg (1624 lbs)
Front suspension	Beam axle, semi-elliptic springs
Rear suspension	Live axle, semi-elliptic springs
Top speed	135 mph
0-60 mph	4.8 seconds

Frazer Nash Le Mans Replica   1949

A good companion

About halfway through my time with the Frazer Nash it occurred to me that there might not be much to write about.

It wasn't blindingly fast - how could it be with a mere 140 horsepower? - and there was no heroic wrestle with the wheel, stomach muscles knotted in a desperate attempt to hold lower body in shiny seat. The four gears snicked in and out with ease and precision if not with lightning speed, while the pedals down below were nice places to rest your feet. They were also right where you expected them to be. The brake was in the middle and it operated hydraulics rather than a web of cables and pulleys.

Frazer Nash Le Mans Replica

The cockpit was inviting too, leather-lined, warm and cosy with a deep hide seat and a nice leather support for the shoulders. Ahead, the driver's aeroscreen was reassuringly tall and through it there was a pleasant view of a curvy bonnet on a curvy body complete with period leather straps and rows of slotted louvres. Wheels were still visible pattering up and down but they were big steel discs, not spokes, and shrouded by vintage motorcycle mudguards with room between them and the body for a pair of podded headlights. Warm air scudded through these restful surroundings carrying a scent of freshly cooked oil. After the upright and exposed cockpits of the 1920s and 30s, this began to feel like a perfect place to sit for 24 hours.

Something that does everything as it should without a struggle might seem less exciting, but it was definitely progress. It almost seemed a shame to provoke such a seemingly honest companion into some kind of retaliation, but in the interests of research, it had to be done. I made my way down the straight, savouring the sound of the sweet six cylinder engine. Right on schedule every time, its smooth hum turned first to a gentle wail then to a subdued ERA-style crackle as the giant tacho in the dash ahead recorded the passing of 4,000 rpm. I lined up for Stowe Corner and trod the middle pedal. A bit more progression and a touch more feel than from the cable-operated variety but not that much in the way of bite from the big drums inside the wheels. A gentle moan of protest from skinny Dunlops says that the rears are slowing more than the fronts. Click, pause and click the stumpy gearlever forward for third gear, feel the slight crunch as vintage synchromesh aligns the gears and... ease the wheel right.

I bought this not so much for myself as for my wife Annette. I wanted her to have a car she could race without humiliating me, and anyway I was starting to run a little low on Astons as my daughters were racing the Ulsters. And issuing team orders and race tactics to a driver line-up consisting solely of blood relatives was a prospect even the McLaren team boss Ron Dennis might have baulked at.

I tend to belong to the school of thought that if you're buying a box of chocolates for someone it seems sensible to choose your favourite centres, and I had always thought of the Frazer Nash as the archetypal British sports car, one that many great drivers, including Stirling Moss, had driven early in their career. This particular model also came highly recommended by many people whose judgment I respected. Neil Corner, Frank Sytner and Sir Anthony Bamford all drive a number of great cars but maintain the Frazer Nash would be one of the very last they'd ever part with.

This car had been owned by Tony Charnock, who had earlier sold me the Jaguar D-Type, and came via a London dealer. I was particularly impressed with the invoice, which indicated that the car was sold as a collector's item and was not necessarily suitable for driving. With this less than confident indication of the car's condition we were still able to get an entire season of racing out of the car with no major overhaul, until we decided this was too much like Russian roulette and got the spanners out.

I think if I'd set out to construct a car from scratch, this is how I'd have liked it to turn out. It is always an immense pleasure to drive, embodying all the characteristics of an old car in its look and feel, but delivering relatively modern performance and comfort. I like to think of it as the mechanical equivalent of a golden retriever.

The four-spoked steering wheel is big like those of its forebears, but the response is much more direct. Just one turn is all you have and the slightest movement brings a prompt retort from the Nash's rounded nose. At first it feels a bit like the Panhard, only with 50 years' progress at the chassis end. At first I was cornering in a series of twitches. Turn too much, unwind, turn again, unwind again, and so on until the corner was done. Then, you learnt to relax. Enter the corner a bit faster and apply pressure rather than movement to the wheel. Funny how so many of these cars seem to tidy their act as soon as you push on... Not that the Frazer Nash need be untidy. Squeeze the wheel's plastic rim and hold the pressure with the shoulders while you push the accelerator. Now you find the engine crackling, revs rising as the inside rear wheel gently prises itself loose from the road. Power is lost and the car slows. Back comes the wheel to earth. Drives again. Gains more speed. Picks up the wheel once more.

Another form of twitching, but equally polite, and the trick to deal with it was becoming familiar. You have to make the car turn with the energy of extra speed and the provocation of brake as much as steering pressure. Perhaps those locking rear wheels were by design after all. As the Frazer Nash yaws gently, discreetly, into the turn, pour on the power progressively and smoothly. Such is the demeanour of the Replica though, that this will only be partially successful. You can attain something approaching a drift, but nothing like as much as with the Lotus or even the ERA, which felt similar but more violent. The amount is always limited by the rear wheel's eventual departure from the road.

This dangling rear wheel acts as some kind of safety valve. Just as a four-wheel Frazer Nash slide is difficult, kicking the back end wide with the right foot is equally hard because at some point your efforts will be frustrated by a spinning wheel and rising engine note. Trying to unstick the other end meets with similar good-natured rebuke. You can enter the corner way too fast but the Nash's front wheels will just gently run wide of the corner. No matter how hard you try and provoke the car, it keeps its temper.

It was the great Jackie Stewart who once remarked that a good racing car should be "a bit of a bitch to drive", but I'm not sure he was right. There's a lot to be said for making the driver's job easy - even if you did have Stewart's talent, but especially if you don't. It is easy to see why so many people liked the Le Mans replica and why it made such a good customer racing car. Its viceless manner made it easy for the fledgling racing driver to practise his or her art in safety - still does - and it was and is simple enough to be maintained by amateurs.

After the Second World War, Frazer Nash's owners, the Aldington brothers, worked with BMW's chief designer Dr Fiedler to create a new two-seater that still retained the stark but rakish feel of the company's pre-war models. When the car appeared at the 1948 Motor Show it was called the 'High Speed', but after H.J. Aldington and Norman Culpan finished third in the following year's Le Mans, establishing the model's reputation, its name was changed to 'Le Mans Replica'.

This Frazer Nash, TMX 543, first appeared in immaculate condition with silver chassis and body (as pictured above) at the 1949 Geneva Motor Show, driven out to Switzerland by W.H. Aldington. The car's first owner, Jack Newton, took it on after the show and had a number of victories with it in the early 1950s, including first in class at the Nürburgring 1000K race in August 1953, driven by Mike Currie.

Frazer Nash Le Mans Replica

Specification

Engine capacity/configuration	1971 cc/6 cylinders in line
Valve gear	Single high camshaft, short pushrods, cross-shaft rockers
Power	140 bhp @ 5750 rpm
Power to weight ratio	101 bhp per ton
Transmission	Rear drive, 4 speed and reverse synchromesh
Tyre sizes	550 x 16 front and rear
Wheelbase	2451 mm (8 ft 0.5 ins)
Track	1270 mm (4 ft 2 ins) front and rear
Brakes	Hydraulic drum
Length	3530 mm (11 ft 7 ins)
Width	1422 mm (4 ft 8 ins)
Height	1041 mm (3 ft 5 ins)
Weight	738 kg (1624 lbs)
Front suspension	Independent, lower wishbones, transverse leaf
Rear suspension	Live axle, torsion bars and 'A' bracket
Top speed	120 mph
0-60 mph	8.9 secs

BRM V16 Mk 2   1953

The impossible dream

Our test of the BRM V16 has a parallel in history. On four separate occasions we attempted to try the car, and each time the car could not complete even a single lap while running properly.

Everyone present, however, marvelled at its meticulous engineering, then winced at the sheer amount of noise it made. From a short time behind the wheel I gained a sense of its potential and it was enough to believe that the car could have been a world-beater. By the end of its development in 1955, the BRM's 16 cylinder one and a half litre engine was producing 600 bhp at 12,000 rpm. As far as we know, this represents the most power per litre from a reciprocating engine until the turbocharged Formula 1 era of the mid-1980s. It was a record that would stand for nearly 30 years.

The sense of frustration at Silverstone must have had its historical parallel too. Time after time the mechanics would beaver away inside that long body, endlessly removing sparking plugs, testing ignition leads, scraping contact points, dismantling the fuel system. Time after time, these items would go back on the engine. I would climb into the roomy cockpit, turn on the tap for the alcohol fuel, flick the single switch for the ignition, find second of the five gears then wait for a push from willing hands eager to see if their perseverance would be rewarded.

The 16 tiny pistons, each of them smaller than those in your lawn mower, whirr through their individual cycles, each one sending a gentle plop down its separate 12-inch stub exhaust pipe before the fire even catches. When it does, the flames come in little groups. First one or two cylinders, then another pair, a quartet, a septet. Each one spits a puff of smoke out of the side exhausts, like a row of shotguns loosing off. Then comes the total.

The noise made by a BRM V16 is one of the most awesome events in motor sporting history. Nothing, but nothing, has made a sound like it, either before or since. It is not just the volume, although that is enough to make even hardened racewatchers cover their ears and grimace in pain, but its sheer intensity. The sound is so much deeper and more multi-layered than the shrill and equally painful scream of a modern Formula 1 engine. The BRM's noise assumes another dimension which you feel as well as hear, like a disco's bass stack played too loud. It's like a whole grid of NASCAR V8 stock cars in concert. It's like a guitar howling round the amplifier loop, like an army of mutant chainsaws out of control. It's all of them together. It rises and falls with the engine's revs, swelling in its intensity while barely changing a note.

I would never have dreamt of going out to buy this car if I hadn't been cajoled by a dealer into believing I was getting a bargain. Smiling like a great white shark he told me he had "something you'd be interested in". I said I doubted it, reaching for my cheque book...

The BRM had been bought by some Greek shipowners who - possibly under the influence of an ouzo overdose - thought that classic racing cars were a good investment. The value of old cars foundered around the same time as their shipping business.

What they had bought into, and what I was being offered, was a major restoration project not a finished car, but the fact that it was with a talented and reputable restorer in the shape of Tony Merrick helped influence my decision to get involved. I can't have had any other cars in pieces at the time, as I've discovered my life is incomplete without at least one vehicle totally dismembered. The BRM ensured a very full life indeed. It was nearly ready to go by BRM standards: just another four years' work. I once made the mistake of working out that the cost per yard travelled was approximately the same as laying the finest Wilton carpet.

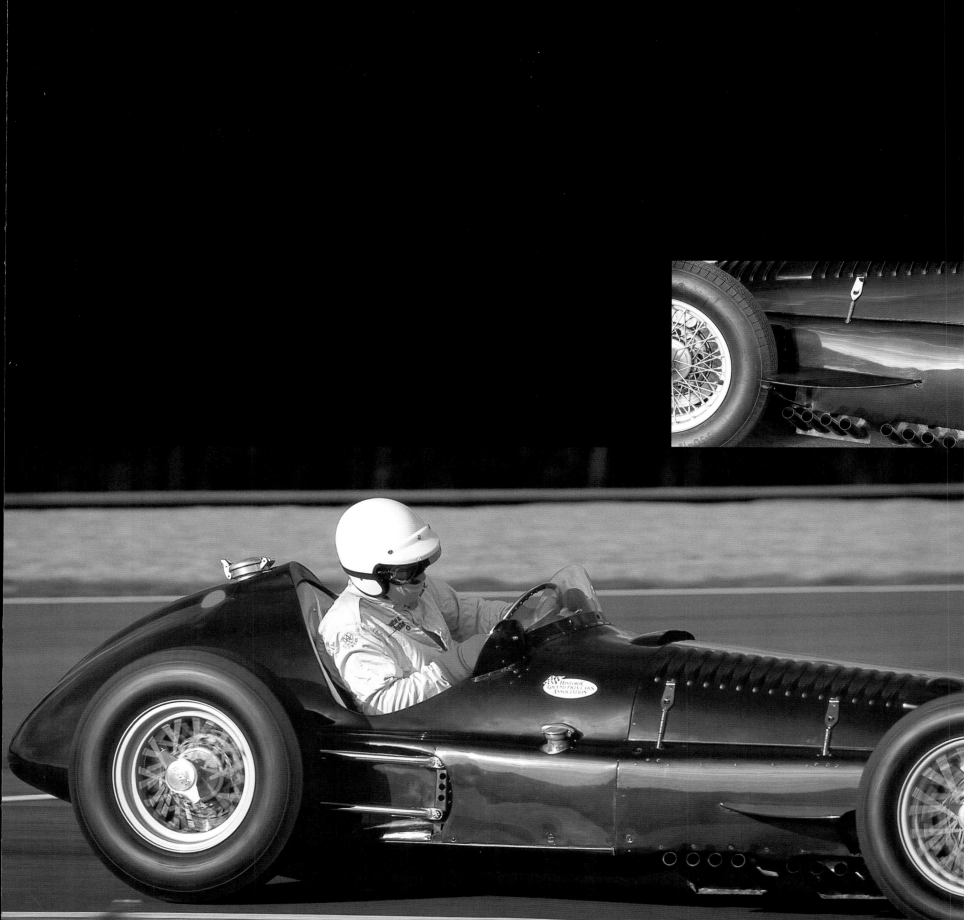

The BRM is still one of the most exotic of all racing cars, a fabulously complicated engineering project, with all the optimistic vision of Victorians trying to build a space rocket. It has 16 jewel-like cylinders and individually hand-machined components, the like of which I didn't see until I went to visit a modern Formula 1 factory.

Without doubt its greatest asset is the sheer noise of the engine: an unmistakeable high-pitched wail. It's extraordinary how much pleasure it can give people.

And yet it is musical. A multi-textured wall of wailing sound that rolls round the countryside for miles, echoing eerily back in the quiet moments when the driver backs off. And here is another strange thing. When you lift from the throttle, there is nothing from those exhausts, not a murmur to drown the gentle whirr of pistons and swish of transmission and tyre. The BRM's soundtrack is a series of giant shrieks broken by silence and the echo rolling back. It is as memorable as it is impossible to describe.

Sadly, the noise-making opportunities were few and far between. I would drive out of the pits, marvelling at the easy clutch and the sweet gearshift down on the floor to my right. Take an exploratory weave at the light and responsive steering and see the gleaming Girling calipers and huge discs beside the front wheels moving in perfect harmony. The engine, which I already know is capable of filling the entire Silverstone area with noise, is humming like a contented cat. Press the pedal. The hum turns gradually to a wail until, at about 6,000 rpm, it suddenly becomes that mountain of vocal energy. Once the needle reaches six, it is as if you have just pulled away from the start in any other car, because six is where the BRM goes to work. From there until 12,000 rpm, the power

output almost doubles with every 2,000 revs. Or at least it did. I could get to about nine by gently coaxing and tickling the accelerator. Then the engine would cut dead as if someone had switched it off. Pull my foot gently from the pedal and the 16 cylinders come back one by two, by four by twelve. Accelerate again and they cut. Too much pedal too soon and they cut.

Various theories abounded. Perhaps the methanol from the big carburettor that feeds the supercharger, designed and made by Rolls Royce, was freezing somewhere between blower and engine. Maybe the vegetable oil that burns with that unique, savoury tang was oiling the plugs. Maybe one or two or three of the four magnetos were shorting inside themselves once the sparks grew too frequent with rising revs. Maybe...

While the toiling mechanics dismantled more beautifuly machined parts in search of an answer, I just stood and looked at this heroic British failure. The engine is hugely long for just 1,496 cc and the angle between the vee of its two banks of cylinders very wide at 135 degrees. The supercharger blower was based on experience gained with the Merlin engine in the Supermarine Spitfire and North American Mustang and is geared to spin at 40,000 rpm. Its case is elaborately machined and lies in front of the engine, with the big variable choke carburettors lying on their sides in front. This mass of machinery looks complex, but according to the engineers, this is nothing compared to the intricacy inside. This, however, is not what strikes me most. Every piece of metal, every bracket, each steering arm, each suspension part, is fashioned and cut from solid pieces of high-quality, corrosion-proof steel. Every bulkhead is elaborately filled with lightening holes, each one with its edges carefully curled to restore the strength. There is no attempt at expediency anywhere, nothing made more simple where it only has to fill a need. The BRM appears to be a complete exercise in labour intensity.

The huge and powerful disc brakes were a feature years before the wonderful Maserati 250F appeared with its huge drums in the mid-1950s, while the BRM was suspended not by steel coils, but by gas and oil struts like an aircraft. These were operated by bellcranks and rods to keep them out of the way. And craftsmen from companies under BRM's guidance made all of this to BRM's specific requirements, as well as the engine, blower, chassis, gearbox... This last piece of crafstmanship lies between the rear wheels, driven by a short propeller shaft like the Maserati's, but the BRM shift is even lighter and more positive. There is not so much as a snick or click to let you know the gears are engaged, but it's not necessary. The gate is easy and accurate and much narrower than that of the Maserati, which would set the standard years later.

We would try just one last time. The engineers removed and soaked the rows of spark plugs in petrol to remove traces of oil, replaced them and gave

Whenever the engine is started up enthusiasts are drawn to it like a magnet, recognising the BRM's voice in the same way an aeroplane-lover can instantly identify the sound of a Merlin-engined Spitfire. The very first time we ran the car at the army's test track at Chobham a retired colonel arrived within minutes, caught up in the nostalgia of seeing the car's first appearance at Silverstone when he'd been a junior officer.

In 1990 Tony was preparing two cars for a demonstration at the British Grand Prix. He realised after three desperate sleepless weeks of engine rebuilds that he was simply experiencing a fraction of the stress that the BRM team suffered for a continuous five-year period. One of the original mechanics explained that when the factory moved on to the four cylinder car it felt like Christmas...

The driving was not much better. Compared to the Alfas and Maseratis of the period it was considerably more demanding with its much narrower rev band, requiring considerable skill to drive competitively. Even Fangio and Moss were fairly unenthusiastic about the car. They respected its power but didn't find it particularly easy to drive, and more importantly they disliked its lack of reliability.

me an immediate push start. I was to drive straight off with the engine under load in the hope that this would make the fires burn hotter and keep the plugs clean. It worked for just half a lap before the stalls started again, but it was enough to see how fast this car could be. So powerful was the engine even in this hesitant half-throttled state that the rear tyres would light up every time the engine passed 6,000, whatever the gear. Every time they smoked and spun, the rear end would dip on those oleo struts and the car would snake and slither. The engine is vastly, ludicrously powerful for a pair of tyres just ten inches wide. But those tyres could rest easy. The engine would not give power for long enough to test them. And yet despite the hiccups and stalls, when we attached the timing equipment, the BRM proved very nearly as quick in acceleration as the 250F.

It was disappointing of course, but surely not so much as when the hopes of a nation rested on this unbelievably complicated, ingenious beast with all its modern features. It boasted rack and pinion steering, disc brakes and five speeds when cars nearly a decade later would have none of these. But even when it did run well, the tyres couldn't cope. Because the horsepower rose so much as the revs climbed, the rubber of the time simply didn't have enough grip to handle it and wheelspin destroyed the tread. If the tyres had been better, if the ignition system had been more advanced. If, if...

A fascinating legacy, nevertheless, and once seen and heard, never forgotten. So sad that such progress and such ingenuity has to go down in history as a failure. The BRM was just way ahead of its time. There. that's a much nicer way to remember it.

I still hope to file a report of victory from the front line, but in the ten years I've owned the BRM, we've rarely had the chance to drive it to the max. When I did compete with it in 1997 I believe this was the first time one had finished a race since 1955; I suspect I was lucky the race was stopped early.

However, this is a wonderful car to own and demonstrate, and does give a sense of helping to contribute to the preservation of a wonderful piece of motoring heritage: the only other V16 BRMs are in the National Motor Museum and Tom Wheatcroft's Donington Collection. Since running the BRM is a constantly frustrating but fascinating battle, with every outing followed by a lengthy period of convalescence, I must give credit to such knowledgeable and supportive allies.

The BRM (British Racing Motors) project involved much of the British motor and accessory industry in carrying the nation's hopes for Grand Prix success after over two decades in the wilderness. The V16 configuration with two-stage centrifugal supercharging had the potential to produce 500 bhp, but unfortunately technical problems were rife. As 350 separate suppliers became involved, difficulties in quality control and delivery inevitably arose through post-war austerity. The car's problems on the track were typified by the Mark 1's failure even to leave the grid on its debut in the 1950 Daily Express Trophy race at Silverstone.

When found to be no quicker than the lightweight Maserati A6GCMs with half the power, Sir Alfred Owen commissioned development engineer Tony Rudd to produce a lighter, shorter Mark 2, including this car, chassis number 2/02. Although the design was perfected too late for the GP formula for which the V16 had been intended, this car had some success in Formule Libre racing with Peter Collins and Ron Flockhart.

BRM V16 Mk 2

Specification	
Engine capacity/configuration	1490 cc supercharged/16 cylinders in vee
Valve gear	4 overhead camshafts
Power	550-600 bhp @ 11500 rpm
Power to weight ratio	522 bhp per ton
Transmission	Rear drive, 5 speed and reverse, non-synchro, rear-mounted transaxle
Tyre sizes	Front: 550 x 16/Rear: 700 x 16
Wheelbase	2349 mm (7 ft 8.5 ins)
Track	Front:1371 mm (4 ft 6 ins)/Rear: 1346 mm (4 ft 5 ins)
Brakes	Hydraulic disc, 6 pot calipers front and rear
Length	3873 mm (12 ft 8.5 ins)
Width	Front: 1574 mm (5 ft 2 ins)/Rear: 1524 mm (5 ft 0 ins)
Height	1041 mm (3 ft 5 ins)
Weight	636 kg (1399 lbs)
Front suspension	Independent, trailing arms, oleo pneumatic struts
Rear suspension	De Dion, oleo pneumatic struts
Top speed	165-170 mph
0-60 mph	3.9 seconds

Jaguar D-Type   1955

Strength in beauty

Every time you walk away from Jaguar's D-Type, you cannot resist at least one backward glance. You have to drink in all those beautiful curves at least once more.

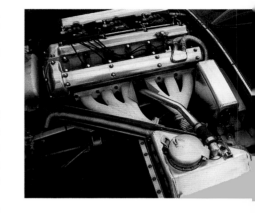

You feel the need to take a last longing look at that curving cockpit with its big wood-rimmed wheel and elaborate fairing behind the driver's head. Who cares that the car's track is narrow and the elaborately perforated disc wheels look too tall, as if the body has been perched on a chassis intended for the next model up? It matters not a bit. Everything flows together as a wonderful, purposeful whole. If the Ferrari GTO has the muscular grace of a feline then the D-Type affects the ruthless beauty of a killer fish.

It was raining when I drove the D-Type for the first time but the exposed cockpit was warm and cosy. There was the cracked and scuffed leather seat and armrest, the solid aluminium cover over the passenger space and the curving windscreen which perfectly met the wrap-around perspex windows. Endless space below for your legs and feet but your head had popped into the cockpit of a biplane fighter from the 1930s. Neither fully open nor properly closed, it was a mixture as seductive as it was unusual.

Nothing strange or complicated about getting the D-Type moving, mind you. One touch of a button and the impressively shiny six cylinder engine which fills most of that swooping bonnet starts after barely half a turn of the clattering starter. After that it will sit and idle with no temperament whatsoever while it warms up.

A couple of laps on a greasy track weren't quite so easy. The steering is so light that you'd swear it was power-assisted. You would, were it not for its intimate feel and immediate willingness to report how well the relationship between front tyres and track surface is going. Meanwhile, the back end is something of a challenge. The tiniest suspicion of a turn and a merest squeeze of power had the rear wheels spinning like crazy and the finned hindquarters of the Jaguar skating sideways. And once you had it all sliding, it was difficult to stop - backing off the power completely was almost as bad as unleashing too much. Whatever you did, the tail yawed ever wider and although the steering was delightful to hold when initiating the turn, that big wheel seemed to take an awful lot of winding when there was need for opposite lock and a prompt cure for an ever increasing slide.

This is the car I'm ashamed to say I never intended to buy. It wasn't on my shopping list even though the D-Type with its Le Mans wins in the mid-1950s was as much a part of my schooldays as grey flannel trousers. In fact my insurance broker persuaded me that maybe I should buy a D-Type on the grounds it might be useful later as part of a package of cars I could swop for a GTO.

This particular D-Type came from Tony Charnock; his father was a noted motoring writer whose work I knew well. The car had also been owned for a time by the Hon. Alan Clark MP, which proves that even Tory politicians have taste. Although the car had no significant racing history other than a brief stint in Florida run by the original owner, a US army commander, the compensation was that the car was pretty well original. An added bonus was finding that all the numbers matched, meaning there would be no wrangling over its genealogy, and that virtually no restoration was required.

The trick, learnt after several scary moments heading for what seemed like an inevitable spin, was not to provoke the car in the first place. Now, while this might sound terribly obvious, the car felt so composed before the event that you always hoped, this time, perhaps it might let you use a little more of that wonderful smooth flow of power. You hoped that last time had been an isolated skiddy patch under the rear wheels and now they might be ready to handle the real thing.

Every time, though, the rear end would skate and the rear wheels would spin. It wasn't snappy and horrible like a car which has been badly set up, it was just the way it was. Soon I learnt to use that willing well of power yet more sparingly and at the same time learnt that whilst I always hoped that the D-Type would not slither wide, it always did, but always in exactly the same fashion and in exactly the same place. As the track dried, the speeds went up but the trend remained entirely consistent. The D-Type may not have the elegant balance of a GTO but it was always supremely predictable.

As a bonus, there was that aforementioned stockpile of power. In a straight line the D-Type was perfect. Perfect for the purpose for which it was designed, which was to compete at Le Mans where the straight is longer than any other. Time after time I savoured that six cylinder howl, that deep-chested boom and bellow followed by a crackle and pop with every carefully managed gearshift. Savoured the quirky gearchange controlled by a short gearlever, cranked so far forward that knuckles punch transmission tunnel when shifting from second to third. A shift which is light but sticky. Pull the lever firmly enough to release it from the gear below and it jerks back and overcomes the synchronisers with a downmarket crunch. Try and ease it out and it takes too long. The engine's revs will have dropped away and you get a learner driver's surge as the clutch pulls them back up again. Better to relax and don't think about it. Tensing the arms only makes it worse.

Safe on the straight and with gearshifting done for a while, I watched the needle-thin pointer on the huge rev counter climb towards 6,000 in the fourth and final ratio. Soothing warm air swirled around my legs and filtered past my chest up into the aircraft cockpit round my helmeted head. Calmed by this wonderful soundtrack and a warm contrast to the freezing British winter just beyond the cockpit's cocoon, a glance at the equally large speedometer was a rude reminder of the forces at work. Surely not 160 mph so soon and so easily.

The D-Type's brake pedal was as light as the steering, but without the feel. The Jaguar's bonnet dips smartly as I tread the foot and the nose wanders right then left. Too much and a front tyre squeals in frozen protest, but this time I get no clues as to when it is about

The only significant modification I can recall was changing the final drive ratio from its Le Mans spec, which made the exercise of moving off at traffic lights a challenge. Far worse, the clutch had to be changed constantly, and after several facefuls of oil and tubfuls of Swarfega I opted for modern clutch materials and lower gear ratios.

Unusually, I had been able to test drive this car before buying it. When I got behind the wheel it won me over immediately. As with all the best cars, it sounded terrific, looked wonderful, had a classic cockpit, and the aspect through the single screen over its sculpted bonnet made me feel instantly like Mike Hawthorn.

I also discovered how easy it is to inspect yourself in large plate-glass windows while driving, though I'd advise only doing so at under 10 mph. The one place not to sit is in the passenger seat. The toolbox underneath the seat raises the occupant some eight inches above the windscreen, which is both uncomfortable and undignified.

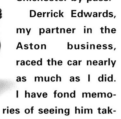

This was easily the most powerful car I'd owned to date, a real step-up after the Astons, and initially its performance was extremely exciting (i.e. alarming). I used to drive the car on the road to various sprints and hill-climbs, which also gave me the opportunity to experiment with its handling characteristics as I spun the car going into a roundabout on the Chichester by-pass.

Derrick Edwards, my partner in the Aston business, raced the car nearly as much as I did. I have fond memories of seeing him taking part in a VSCC driving test, sailing across a stop line - and past some surprised stewards - with the wheels locked, at speed, having had a bit too much fun with the acceleration.

Shortly after buying the D-Type I did manage to acquire a GTO. Thank goodness the seller was not interested in part exchanges, leaving me with one of the nicest cars of all.

to happen. I would have to build a rhythm and take my cues from the circuit rather than the car. But for now the fact that the brakes are as tireless as the chassis is loyal is welcome help. I need to take note of the fact that this car has over 250 horsepower and tyres little wider than those fitted to the Bugatti of 1927. The Jaguar's steadfast character - and perhaps more important, its 24-hour stamina - comes not least from its simplicity of construction. Its big beam of a back axle, which might bring about a premature slither and slide but which does without a quartet of potentially fragile universal joints. Its wonderful, smooth 3.4 litre engine, which wails and gargles while producing seamless power from just above tickover. Coughing in protest if you tread the accelerator too quickly before bellowing loud and clear on time every time. The body's shark-like shape, which may not be the ultimate in aerodynamic efficiency, but which is so stable as to be almost soporific even at three miles a minute.

The D-Type was simple and strong, massively fast down the straight and tireless everywhere. All its controls were effortless to operate, which placed less physical demand on the driver - an essential in the days when drivers had been known to party as long and late as the race that followed. If the passage of time is to highlight any shortcoming in the D-Type, it is grip in corners, but that is not entirely the car's fault. The D-Type made effective if not elegant use of the tyre technology of the day while concentrating on other strengths necessary for a 24-hour contest. The Jaguar engineers knew perfectly well how to design independent rear suspension, but opted for a truck's beam axle because it was simpler and stronger. Despite this and as Nick knows full well, it would certainly be possible to improve his D-Type's handling by making some changes to suit today's rubber. That though, would be to miss the point. The D-Type was perfect for the job for which it was designed and once you had your head back in the 1950s, was a very English delight. It should be left exactly as it is.

The successor to the C-Type - Jaguar's first true competition car, designed by Bill Heynes and which had won Le Mans in 1951 and 1953 - the D-Type was created with the single aim of further victory there. The design focus was on strength, reliability and aerodynamics to optimise performance on Le Mans' high-speed straights: the team brought in the C-Type aerodynamicist Malcolm Sayer specifically to develop the car's flowing lines.

After a disappointing second place behind Ferrari in 1954, the D-Type triumphed the following year after a tremendous battle between Mike Hawthorn and Ivor Bueb in the D-Type and Fangio and Moss in a Mercedes. This D-Type, chassis number XKD 516, is one of just over 40 production variants. Its first owner, the American John Rutherford, raced the car at Nassau and Daytona, before it returned to Britain in 1973.

Jaguar D-Type

Specification

Engine capacity / configuration	3442 cc / 6 cylinders in line
Valve gear	Double overhead camshafts
Power	250 bhp @ 5750 rpm
Power to weight ratio	244 bhp per ton
Transmission	Rear drive, 4 speed and reverse synchromesh
Tyre sizes	Front: 550 x 16 / Rear: 600 x 16
Wheelbase	2298 mm (7 ft 6.5 ins)
Track	Front: 1270 mm (4 ft 2 ins) / Rear: 1219 mm (4 ft 0 ins)
Brakes	Hydraulic discs with power assistance
Length	3911 mm (12 ft 10 ins)
Width	1651 mm (5 ft 5 ins)
Height	820 mm (2 ft 8 ins)
Weight	992 kg (2182 lbs)
Front suspension	Independent, double wishbones, torsion bars
Rear suspension	Live axle, torsion bars, radius arms, 'A' bracket
Top speed	170 mph
0-60 mph	6.3 seconds

Maserati 250F   1957

A profile so perfect

This would be the special one. Long before I became passionate about driving race cars, this was the car. This was the shape doodled by generations of schoolboys, because it was what a real racing car looked like.

A long bonnet and high tail, smooth curves and not a straight panel in sight. A profile so perfect it could only have been fashioned by the hand of genius. A profile that was perfect yet looked awkward in any colour but red. And ever since I too drew those same shapes on my school exercise book, years before I ever set foot in a competition car, I had dreamed of driving a 250F.

This time, though, I just knew the experience would match the shape. It wouldn't be like the Bugatti - an interesting insight but coming from such a different age that any current experience was almost redundant. No, all those people over the years couldn't be wrong about the 250F. The great Fangio, gifted as he was with unnatural ability, could not have done it unaided at the Nürburgring in 1957. Could not have drifted past the camera to provide that once-in-a-century image, that summary of what a 250F could do when guided by a special pair of hands. For a mere mortal like me, driving the 250F would be akin to a religious experience.

There would, as well, be an earthly content to this experience. Since those schooldays, I have spent some time learning how to drive race cars and I wanted to know how Fangio and his contemporaries kept that drift going for so long. The early cars like the ERA and Bugatti had allowed glimpses, but their frames were too flexible and their suspension too simple to let it go on and on.

The 250F's cockpit is roomy but intended mainly for those short of leg and the minimal seat is comfortable but not remotely likely to hold you in place. Gearlever is right down on the floor to your right and at first needs a search every time to locate. It controls a gearbox which offers five speeds rather than the four of previous generations and which lies between the rear wheels, taking its drive via a propeller shaft which spins at engine speed. I try not to think about the fact this passes just inches beneath my seat. The steering wheel, with the elegant marquetry of its wooden rim, is a much more reassuring feature, so large it spans almost the entire width of the cockpit. The wheel is so very visible no matter at what angle you survey the car, and it somehow looks like some central master control, as if it governs more than just the

This is the car that has been appreciated by the great, the good and the really rather average. Capable of winning World Championships in its heyday, the 250F has been providing great racing experience for three generations of drivers. I'd had some involvement with this period of racing car when I owned an A-type Connaught - a delightful car but not a front runner - and had sat on the start-line gazing with envy down the exhaust pipes of the 250Fs lined up on the front of the grid.

The 250F eventually forced itself on me, but I willingly offered my arm up for twisting. As part of the deal to buy the ERA, the 250F arrived in the form of a basket-case of bits as a compulsory add-on. I was happy to take on the task of reconstruction with what was fast being a regular excuse that this was a cheap way of acquiring a car.

The rebuild was slow. The first task after completing the deal was to rescue the car from a restorer who had run out of ideas and money and was in danger of selling off the parts. Then, with the help of Rick

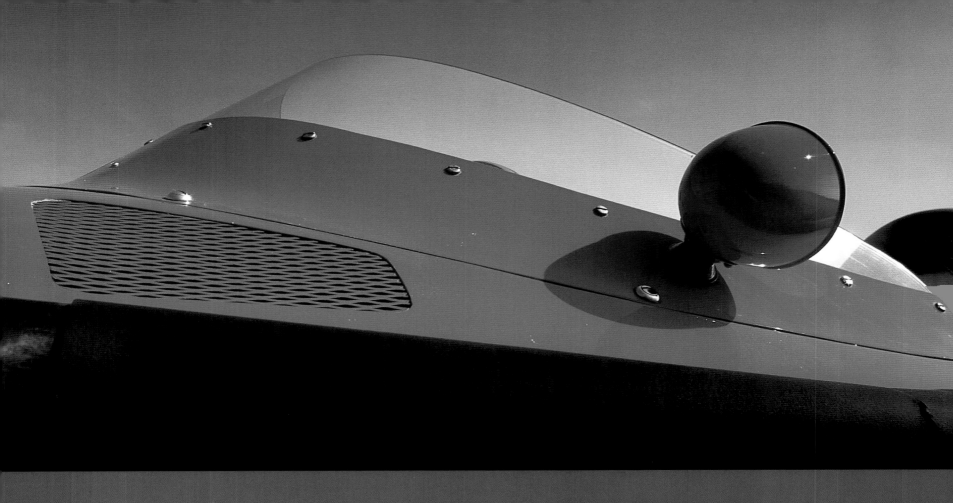

angle of the front wheels. Only later did the science of ergonomics dictate smaller steering wheels, mounted at the end of a long column and with the dash a long way distant. With this change a whole style of cockpit was altered.

The Grand Prix starting handle had already gone, though, and there's no starter motor or even any generator to feed any electrics. The engine's magnetos are the only electrical items on the car and are completely self-contained. Mechanics puff and pant as they roll the Maserati forward, trying always to find a convenient handhold amongst all those curves. Clonk as the silvery gearlever slips into second, up with the clutch and I'm away. The boom and crackle from that long exhaust running under my elbow is there the very instant the clutch is home, shatteringly loud, yet immediately addictive. The tremor beneath the clutch foot and the little jingling noise which comes and goes with the revs serves as a reminder of the energy running through that long propshaft.

Once it's all together and driving hard, the six cylinder engine is totally smooth and once your reach down to the floor is confident the gearchange is effortless. It shifts as fast as you can move the lever with the merest click and crunch - just enough to let you know the gears are engaged - and the only bit of technique that needs to be mastered is remembering the width of the slotted gate. You move the lever as far across as you do back and forward. So far, it's all as I imagined.

My upper body is exposed and my overalls are gently ruffled by the slipstream. There's no roll cage and no belts, just like the cockpits of the early cars, but this time I feel less vulnerable. That big wheel gives a feeling of personal security as well as exerting masterly control over the whole car. Its action is not feather light like the D-Type's or the T61 Birdcage sports car, nor is it telepathic like the GTO's. It needs a firm grip with effort from the shoulders as well as biceps, but you never need to search for a response like you do with more modern cars. Not that the car feels nervous or twitches in answer to the slightest movement, but you always feel confident that it will control the car.

This is partly thanks to an accurate set of messages coming back via the rim. The car rolls quite a lot for a single seater, but as it does, the amount of effort needed to hold the lock varies accordingly. It changes, too, when the car starts to push wide at the front or slew its tail. There are other cars in this book which have communicative steering, but there are none where you can also watch the front wheels moving. The 250F's elevated seating position adds an extra sense to the whole driving process. You can see how much the car is pushing or sliding by looking at the angle between body and front tyre, check how much it is rolling by eyeballing the angles between suspension wishbones and wheelrim.

Hall and Rob Fowler, we established that there was a real car there, although it eventually went to Peter Shaw of Intertech Engineering to complete the task of reassembly. Additional confusion arose because - as it turned out - some parts were for a slightly later model and for a while it was like trying to complete a jigsaw with the pieces from two completely different puzzles.

The car had spent some time in South America and, to avoid some particularly irksome bureaucracy, is said to have come out on the shipping bill described as 'a ladder'. This route was not unusual since at the end of the European season teams often took their cars to South America, where they were eagerly snapped up by buyers for local racing. With a shortage of spares and expertise, the original engines were frequently removed and replaced by the local Chevrolet dealer, which is why on rare occasions it has been possible to find an Italian Grand Prix engine powering a Chevrolet pick-up.

For the professional the car is well balanced and reliable, qualities that make it a great drive for the amateur. On a mechanical level, the car is relatively simple and robust, with very little adjustment available. The engine can often last for two or three years without a major overhaul. The fact the car has a real wood-rimmed steering wheel with alloy spokes, and a rather natty chain for adjusting the radiator blind, also creates one of the best-looking cockpits in motor sport.

Maserati 250F

After a number of sleepless nights Peter Shaw was able to roll the car out of the workshop in time for it to run in the historic car race at Monaco in 1981, with Willie Green at the wheel. Untried and untested (the car, that is), Willie drove it beautifully. I was in the ERA and can honestly say this was one of the rare occasions when I didn't mind being overtaken, as I watched him powering the 250F to third place overall.

It's not something you do consciously, but like a needle out of place on a gauge, you have an automatic sense of what's going on without having to read it too carefully. You also realise how much you are fidgeting with the wheel just to keep the car on line through the corners. And every time you look over your shoulder to check for other traffic, you catch a glimpse of the rear suspension rising and falling and the driveshafts angling and sliding as the 250F rides the road. And still I feel secure.

But what of that four-wheel drift. So far, I have been driving comfortably round, leaning the Maserati into the corners, watching and feeling the push from the front end, then savouring the sliding tail on exit, listening to the revs rise as the body dips towards one front corner and pulls the inside rear wheel from the road, letting it spin in response to that wailing, crackling surge of power. This however is all ordinary stuff. How did Fangio raise the game to a higher level...?

The easy bit is to trust the car. You use the steering's confidence to enter the corner that little bit faster than you previously felt able. More than the front tyres had so far been able to cope with. Use the slight imbalance as you release the brake pedal, take advantage of the tail which has lifted as you slowed, then squeeze the throttle pedal as you ease the wheel towards the turn. The tail will slew immediately to one side and you need a flick of opposite lock to catch it. An exaggerated flick because you want to nab the slide but you don't want the car to straighten up. You want it to keep turning. This is the most critical phase because now you must keep the power pouring on. Not so much that the drift develops into another tail-out slide, but enough to keep the tail sliding just a little.

If you enter the turn just fast enough, if you have collected the first, initial movement of the tail with finesse, and if you have remembered to straighten up the steering, then the chassis will also have settled back to a level attitude. Because the body, with its weight of engine upfront, is no longer leaning on that outside front wheel, the opposite rear will not be pulled rudely from the road and if you have judged the amount of power just so, it will spin only a little and keep driving the car.

It's difficult to do every time, because a lot of things have to be right, and like juggling a number of balls, the start is critical. Get just one of the ingredients slightly wrong - or lose confidence halfway through the corner - and the whole thing just fades away. Either that or you crash. Get it right, and the driving and steering effort will be distributed amongst all four tyres which no longer have to work in separate pairs, but can operate as a quartet.

Modern suspension design and lower centres of gravity have removed the need for this kind of thing, added to which a modern slick tyre would overheat in just a couple of corners. Just occasionally, you see the very best of today's crop using these techniques to wring more from an ill-handling car or deal with a wet road, but they know it's only as long as the tyres will let them. The likes of Fangio and Moss used artistry instead of athleticism and the 250F was the tool that allowed them to display it perfectly. It allowed them to select which of the car's characteristics they needed and in what proportion, and then to mix them together as only they could.

The 250F was everything I expected. It involved you in every part of the driving process without making huge demands but allowed you to move to a higher level if you were capable. A perfect combination and one which technology has denied the drivers of today.

The Maserati 250F made motor racing history at the 1954 Argentine Grand Prix, where Fangio triumphed, and the car became one of the few to win its very first race. By 1957, Maserati had produced the 'Lightweight' 250F works cars, responsible for the marque's most successful season. The company were due to introduce a V-12 engine, but because of financial difficulties they pulled out of Grand Prix racing in 1958. However, they built one final version of the 250F, shorter, smaller and lighter, known as the 'Piccolo'.

It was originally thought that this car, chassis number 2532, was the first of three Piccolos built as unofficial factory cars, but it is now fairly clear that it was the last of a trio of 1957 V-12s subsequently modified to accept six cylinder engines and run in the National Brazilian Formule Libre series. After returning to the UK and being rebuilt the car has been raced extensively at historic car events, as well as being demonstrated by such great drivers as 1961 World Champion Phil Hill (picture above).

Maserati 250F

Specification	
Engine capacity/configuration	2493 cc/6 cylinders in line
Valve gear	Twin overhead camshafts
Power	218 bhp @ 8000 rpm
Power to weight ratio	352 bhp per ton
Transmission	Rear drive, 5 speed and reverse, non-synchro, rear-mounted transaxle
Tyre sizes	Front: 550 x 16 / Rear: 650 x 16
Wheelbase	2280 mm (7 ft 6 ins)
Track	Front: 1360 mm (4 ft 6 ins) / Rear: 1355 mm (4 ft 5 ins)
Brakes	Hydraulic drum
Length	4343 mm (14 ft 3 ins)
Width	1473 mm (4 ft 10 ins)
Height	1054 mm (3 ft 6 ins)
Weight	630 kg (1386 lbs)
Front suspension	Independent, double wishbones, coil springs
Rear suspension	De Dion, transverse leaf spring
Top speed	160 mph
0-60 mph	4.3 seconds

Maserati T61   1959

A collection of tubes

Three litres is a lot to squeeze into just four cylinders. They idle grumpily, popping and spitting through the carburettors. Tap the throttle pedal, though, and the torque rocks the whole car.

Hear the bass heavy thud of a side exhaust. Feel the tingle of four big thrashing pistons massaging the body. It's gruff and tough, but somehow the sound doesn't match the look. The car's foundation is a delicate, filigree collection of tubes, tiny pipes of metal, feeding loads across complex geometry, covered with a body so smooth and curvy it could be melting ice.

It all looks so fragile that you test everywhere with a prod of the boot before committing any weight. Then, once installed, you feel as if you're sitting in some experimental kind of aircraft, surrounded by a fuselage of stressed pipework and four camel humps to cover those tall spoked wheels. Splay the knees to clear the bottom of the big wood-rimmed steering wheel. Screw up the eyes to dim the flash of sun on polished spokes. Feel the metal-on-metal snick of the gear-lever in the gate as you pull the stubby lever with its shiny aluminium knob to the left and back. Ease the car out of the pits.

Snick second. The lever moves in the gate so swiftly and easily it's hard to imagine the mechanism at the other end. Then a squeeze of the throttle pedal and the car is there. The needle on the huge rev counter flicks into the red almost as quickly as it would with the gearlever in neutral. Click third gear and squeeze again. The rush is just as inevitable but the gear is taller and you have a little time to separate the various strands of noise and resonance. First a deep thrum zings through everything, blurring the mirrors, tickling the whole body. Exhaust booms with a breathy, amplified, electric bass rumble, climbing the scale like a finger sliding swiftly up a fretless neck. Then a smooth patch where the reflection in the mirrors comes into focus. Then another vibro band, a higher frequency this time to match the rising revs. A different tickle through the wheel's rim, a lesser blur of the mirrors. More exhaust boom. An amount of noise rather than a volume. It doesn't seem so loud while you're there but it leaves the ears numb for the evening to follow.

The Birdcage's engine has so much muscle and the car is so light that it hardly seems to matter which gear you use. Third, or fourth, will do for most of Silverstone's corners and the engine will always sweep you out of the bend with equal ease. Often you find yourself changing up early - just before the corner - to save the need to shift halfway through and make sure of keeping to the strict 6,500 rpm limit. It doesn't feel right, but it doesn't matter. The engine's torque gets the job done. Progress is all so easy that the Birdcage doesn't feel as quick as it really is.

I can't remember whether I ever actually saw Stirling Moss driving the Birdcage in its heyday, or whether it was from photos, but I have a strong mental picture of the great man behind the wheel, using the classic straight-armed style that the T61 encourages because it's so light to drive. You don't need biceps like Popeye's to keep the Birdcage on the road.

The car itself always looked incredibly exotic, with its swooping curves, and this was what really led me into buying one - well actually two... I bought a T60 first, but it arrived as a box of spare parts, in need of resurrection rather than restoration. Meanwhile another Birdcage, a T61 I'd seen racing, turned up in Italy as a complete car. I persuaded myself that I could decide later on which one to keep; inevitably I still have both.

The T61 was, I was told by the seller, ready to run. Unfortunately in used car parlance 'ready to run' meant 'assembled, but on the verge of collapse'. Although the car's

Maserati T61

marvellous features were intact, the engine was on its last legs and there were more cracked tubes than not. Within a short space of time I had two completely disassembled Birdcages.

It was a bonus to discover the pleasure of driving both the T60 and the T61 once they had been put back together: superb handling, terrific brakes - light years ahead of a car like the 250F - and one of the smoothest gearboxes I've come across on any car of any era.

There are some technical problems involved in running a Birdcage. All those tube joints need frequent checking and, if they're cracked, re-welding: one damaged tube can put a lot of extra strain on the transmission and running gear. In fact a welding kit is an absolute necessity since it's often quicker to remove a tube and replace it than spending hours fiddling about trying to get a spanner through the lattice-work of tubes. It's a mechanic's nightmare - getting your hand inside is difficult, extracting it with the right part nigh on impossible.

But the ability to get the job done whatever the gear also depends on the chassis. The cage of tubing was designed to save weight while lending strength but legend has it that the whole lot would twist and bend. Tubes would crack and welds would break and part of the joy in maintaining a T61 was the welding practice between races. Bendy or not, the Birdcage is a joy to drive, and the next surprise after the sheer punch of the engine is the brakes. In 1960 the T61 had huge discs all round and with little mass to haul back they are powerful and tireless in any terms, let alone for a 35-year-old car. They also allow you to place the car really accurately on entry to the corner which is a big factor in a smooth fast lap.

Ease the big wheel towards the corner. It's easy and light, not perhaps the precision instrument that I would later find in the GTO, but responsive nonetheless. But the T61's answer to the command comes first from the tail. The rear corner sits down a couple of inches and the car takes a set towards the apex. This is the invitation. Ignore it and the car will push relentlessly wide and shun the command. Accept it straightaway and a whole range of possibilities opens up.

Squeeze the throttle pedal and that initial set turns into a distinct yaw. The whole car takes up a skewed angle as the tail sits even further down, while gently stepping wide of the cornering line. Then, you need to straighten up the wheel, either back to neutral or with perhaps a touch of opposite if you were a bit too eager with the accelerator. Now, hold it there, and keep adjusting, either with a merest touch of lock or a slight squeeze of power, remembering as always that the whole process will only keep going if you keep your confidence.

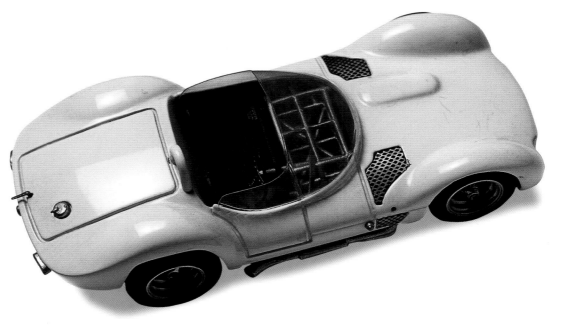

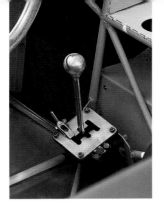

Maserati T61

I have always liked the legend that whenever a Birdcage chassis was being assembled at the Maserati works, the engineers would put a canary inside it; they knew the chassis was finished when the canary stopped escaping. It must have been an apocryphal story, or one hell of a large canary...

By the time I bought the two Birdcages in the 1980s, there had been a resurgence of good sports car racing in Europe, and the Birdcage had emerged as a cult classic. Previously many of the cars had drifted over to the States, since that was where the good racing could be found - proof that this is a driver's car, rather than a collector's folly.

The Birdcage is certainly a joy to drive, and I will always be grateful to it for giving me the race of my career, with a win in the historic sports car race before a packed Grand Prix crowd at Silverstone in 1993. Driving the T60, I managed to steal first place from a couple of D-Type Jaguars on the last corner of the final lap. A moment like that is guaranteed to endear you to a car for life.

It's not like correcting a sudden slide where the tail has kicked out in mid-corner and needs slapping back so you can get on with it, and it's not really like a four wheel drift. More like steering a boat, you need to plan ahead and unlike some later cars which had to be unbalanced with excess speed, you can't use momentum to get the Birdcage drift going because there is not enough bite at the front. Instead you must use the big four cylinder engine's booming reserves of torque. And then just unbalancing the Birdcage with power is not enough either. Too much opposite lock with a great bootful of power is possible - which it wasn't with the 250F - and the T61 will be spectacular yet slow. You have to be going forwards rather than sideways. But on the other hand, not enough power and the car will push on with a vengeance. Whatever, there seems to be plenty of time to adjust and experiment.

There's another odd thing you discover here too. The yaw seems to have a natural duration. Whether it's the Birdcage's bendy chassis unravelling itself or whether energy dissipates as the corner unfolds is difficult to say, but as you near the exit you find it possible to accelerate harder and harder and gradually straighten the wheel. One final thing. Always leave about three feet spare on the exit. As the T61 straightens up, it sort of gathers itself, like a bike racer settling back in the saddle as the bike comes vertical: the Birdcage always seems to move three feet to one side as you straighten up. All too easy to find a wheel the wrong side of the kerb.

Surprisingly, the Maserati Birdcage is faster than the 250F Grand Prix car of three years before, mainly because it gets its power to the road so much more effectively. It is also much less physical to drive. Where the single-seater demands muscular action, the sports racer does most of the work for you. The T61 laid on the most delicious combination of punchy engine, vintage drift, responsive steering and single seater lightness and did it all in the most relaxed and comfortable manner. Every time you moved the wheel, something rather pleasant happened. Of the 21 cars, the Birdcage was probably my ultimate favourite.

Maserati T61

Specification

Engine capacity / configuration	2890 cc / 4 cylinders in line
Valve gear	Twin overhead camshafts
Power	240 bhp @ 6500 rpm
Power to weight ratio	407 bhp per ton
Transmission	Rear drive, 5 speed and reverse, non-synchro, rear-mounted transaxle
Tyre sizes	Front: 550 x 16 / Rear: 650 x 16
Wheelbase	2200 mm (7 ft 3 ins)
Track	Front: 1250 mm (4 ft 1 in) / Rear: 1200 mm (3 ft 11 ins)
Brakes	Hydraulic disc
Length	3780 mm (12 ft 5 ins)
Width	1500 mm (4 ft 11 ins)
Height	916 mm (3 ft 0 ins)
Weight	600 kg (1320 lbs)
Front suspension	Independent, double wishbones, coil springs
Rear suspension	De Dion, twin radius arm, transverse leaf
Top speed	145 mph
0-60 mph	5.8 seconds

Lotus 18   1961

The lightness of speed

The Lotus 18 of 1961 came only four years after the Maserati 250F and yet it might have been the product of a different planet.

Park one against the other and the green insect body of the Lotus will barely reach the tops of the Maserati's wire wheels. The Lotus's four cylinder 2.5 litre engine is behind rather than in front of the driver and because there's no transmission in the cockpit or propeller shaft running front to rear, you can sit lower. Your shoulders will be level with the tops of the wheels because your backside is just six inches above the track, your body relaxed and reclined, arms outstretched. Only the head remains mobile. Drivers of the day soon had their own distinctive style of movement and set of helmet to suit a particular corner. It was an individual expression that would quickly become familiar.

Despite its size, climbing in the Lotus is easy. You step on the seat and then lower yourself on outstretched arms, taking care to make sure you have placed hands on something solid. The detachable fibreglass body is flimsy and easily broken. Reclining in the seat is as comfortable as it sounds and, because you lie back, your stomach muscles don't have to support the torso, and what looks like a shallow bucket holds you very firmly. And there's plenty of room left; the age of racing cars built only for jockey-sized drivers was still some time in the future. Your arms and elbows are free to move without hitting anything and you can easily reach the gearlever, which lies handily at arm's length just to the left of the seat. There's also the reassuring luxury of seat belts to strap you to the machinery. Ahead of you is a tiny thin red-rimmed steering wheel and ahead of that is a screen which wraps round and tapers down the cockpit sides. You already feel like an integral part of the car.

Press the starter and the engine bursts into life not six inches behind you. The exhaust noise stays way out behind but what you can hear is not as rich and interesting as some of the cars with more cylinders. A big four makes a flat bark, enlivened only by the cascading, intestinal crackle from a short open exhaust as you cut power and wheels drive engine. Closer and more audible was the hoarse gobbling noise from the four carburettor intakes as air is sucked into the engine, and the ticking and clicking from the valves and camshafts on the engine's head. Response to the featherweight accelerator is instant: the chronometric tachometer with its filigree needle flicks round half the scale in an instant, then settles back in steps, like a stalking spider.

With the Lotus 18 I was trying to anticipate what the next really good category of historic racing car would be, but having owned a number of Lotus road cars over the years and having had to resort to the services of the AA on a number of occasions, I had mixed feelings about driving the Formula 1 version. However the dealer's patter yet again worked its charms, along with the fact that the car (in pieces) seemed to be a genuine bargain and that Stirling Moss had had one of his greatest-ever races in a Lotus 18. One day I hope to recognise that this tell-tale combination of signs foretells immense expenditure of time and money.

The vehicle arrived from the States, regrettably with fewer pieces than when dispatched, including the disappearance of one very rare set of carburettors. Eventually replacements were found, but it was still some three years before the Lotus was finally ready to run. If anyone sees a New York stevedore in a Pontiac sporting an unusual set of Weber 58DC03s, please let me know.

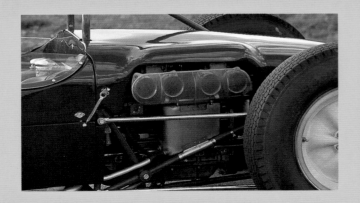

Lotus 18

On its arrival I sent the Lotus straight down to Cedric Selzer, the Team Lotus mechanic who prepared cars for Jim Clark. Cedric's immense experience and knowledge of the car is extremely valuable since it contains a particularly unusual gearbox, manufactured by Lotus themselves and affectionately known by one and all as the 'queer box'. This short-lived experiment lasted until Lotus realised it was really much easier to pop down the road and buy a ready-made unit.

The delay in rebuilding the car was not really a problem, as the enthusiasm I'd anticipated for early rear-engined cars took a long time to get off the ground. The cars proved, quite rightly, to be less than welcome in the races for front-engined cars for the simple reason that they are generally faster; the very reason that rear-engined cars had revolutionised motor racing in just over 12 months in 1959/60. They unfairly made the earlier cars look rather old and cumbersome.

Like most Lotuses the 18 reflects Colin Chapman's philosophy of building racing cars as close to the edge as possible, sacrificing everything for lightness, and hence speed. The theory was, and remains, that the car should fall to pieces 100 yards after the finish line although Lotus had a reputation for sometimes getting this particular sum drastically wrong.

Nevertheless, the Lotus, like the ERA, is a thoroughbred racing car. That's how I like to remember the car, running in races at Goodwood in the early 1960s, and especially Stirling Moss at the wheel of Rob Walker's privately entered Lotus 18 when, driving at ten tenths, he succeeded in remaining ahead of the two works Ferraris of Peter Collins and Phil Hill to win the 1961 Monaco Grand Prix.

What the engine lacks in the aural department, it certainly makes up in the tactile. At first the vibration takes your breath away. Not only are you strapped to the machinery, but the engine feels as if it's strapped to you. Four big cylinders thrum and buzz, tingling through the whole car, blurring the reflection in the wing mirrors and trembling the needles on the gauges. The reverberation tickles your lungs and makes you cough, and later I wondered why my jaws ached. It wasn't from laughing with pleasure, but from grinding teeth in an attempt to calm the chest.

While I huff like a 40-a-day man and the engine warms, I get a greater sense that the Lotus actually is as light as it looks. Flex the wrists and the front wheels, which stand upright and tall and in full view of your line of sight, move immediately and easily and in direct proportion to the tiniest turn of the leather rim. Accurate as well as easy. There was no possible way you could do that while at rest in any of the others.

The five-speed gearbox is way out behind the engine, connected to a stubby gear lever by a long tubular rod. There is no gate as such; instead, the lever moves forward to shift up and back to shift down, which means it will only ever allow you to select the next gear in the sequence - either up or down. It was designed to stop drivers finding fourth instead of second when shifting up or worse, finding second instead of fourth when shifting down. Not only would that risk spinning the Coventry Climax engine to infinity but if you were preparing for a corner it would seize the rear wheels and spin you off as surely as if you had yanked on a handbrake.

Time to go. The Lotus moves easily in response to its featherweight controls and the engine surges the car forward as if some giant force is connected directly to the accelerator. It slows as quickly as it goes and, whatever the gear, the slightest squeeze brings the feel of a big fist in the back. Relax the foot and the fist disappears as quickly as it came. There were other cars of Nick's which could accelerate more quickly, but the response of the Lotus - the way in which it accelerated - was still surprising. A big engine which pulls like a train from tickover, installed in a light car, has always been the best recipe for a feeling of absolute power.

The slipstream swirled and buffeted through the cockpit, punching and roaring against my helmet. A reminder that this was a small body close to the ground. The steering, meanwhile, was every bit as sensitive on the track as it promised in the paddock. The slightest movement made the car dart as if the whole front end had shifted bodily a couple of feet across the track. It was all too easy to fight the wheel and provoke the car, then overcorrect the dive in one direction and replace it with one the opposite way. Added to which the steering itself was constantly coming back at you with a twitch that jarred the wrists if you rode a kerb, with a tug as the grip changed under the front wheels or the car's body rolled. It was informative, possibly welcome, but brash and insistent in a way that the Ferrari GTO wasn't.

95

It was time to practise a new technique. The steering may have been darty, but once into the corner the car would actually push its nose gently wide of the apex. You could see yourself applying a touch of extra lock as the front wheels swivelled and pattered up and down over the bumps. Then suddenly, one rear wheel would unload, the Climax would speed up as the tyre began to spin and the car would twitch its tail sideways in a flash. The steering was all too ready to catch the slide but it was all too easy to turn it too far and give yourself a similar but opposite problem. Smooth driving was part of the answer, but the Lotus also offered other solutions.

This was the advent of the adjustable racing car. Where the Maserati driver simply had to try harder, the Lotus engineers could make adjustments to cure a problem or suit a driver's preference. With the benefit of a lunchtime's reflection and a few clicks softer on the dampers, the Lotus was less snappy and the driver more relaxed. It was easier, and faster, but more importantly I realised once again that waiting for the car to announce its limit by stepping out of line and then for me to correct it was not the fastest way.

Despite its mid-mounted engine, this Lotus was still from a time when tyre grip was limited and cars could be drifted through a bend at an angle, neither pointing nose in or tail out. The technique from now on had to be practised with wrists rather than biceps. The trick was to enter the bend at a high enough speed that the tyres would slide rather than turn - but then to balance the car so it remained under your control. Just enough accelerator kept the tail sliding so that you didn't need any lock to keep the car on line. Too much and the tail would go wide, too little power or too slow an entry to the bend and the nose would push on. The discipline might have been similar to what went before but the manner in which it was achieved was subtly different.

The Maserati was a relatively heavy front-engined car and it gave you an option to get a drift going

and then lost interest if you didn't take it. The Lotus offered a light chassis with the major masses closer to the centre and a set of controls which responded instantly. This revolutionary layout's extra agility allowed the good guys another dimension of authority and a chance to get ever closer to the limit. At the same time it left them in no doubt that a mistake would be firmly and swiftly punished.

The Lotus and its ilk ushered in a golden age when we could watch the artistry of yesteryear using the technology of tomorrow. In another ten years, wings would appear and bring aerodynamic downforce and slick tyres would provide previously impossible amounts of grip. The responsibility of extracting extra speed on the day would shift forever from the cockpit to the workshop.

The first rear-engined Lotus, the 18, was Colin Chapman's response to the success of Jack Brabham's works Coopers, which had grabbed the World Championship in 1959. The 18 was produced in three versions: an 1100 cc Formula Junior, a one and a half litre Formula 2, and the two and a half litre Formula 1, which made its debut at the 1960 Argentine Grand Prix. In 1960 Innes Ireland gave Lotus their first Formula 1 win in the Glover Trophy at Goodwood and Stirling Moss drove his Rob Walker team car to victory in the Monaco Grand Prix, the marque's first 'Grande Epreuve' triumph.

This Lotus 18 - chassis number 909 - was supplied new in 1961 to British Hill Climb champion Tony Marsh. He competed with the car in the 1961 British (picture below) and German Grands Prix, and lent it to Willy Mairesse for the Belgian Grand Prix that same year. This period was the beginning of the end for most of the privateers, as thereafter the costs - and the politics - of running a Grand Prix car escalated.

Lotus 18

Specification

Engine capacity/configuration	2495 cc/4 cylinders in line
Valve gear	Twin overhead camshafts
Power	250 bhp @ 7000 rpm
Power to weight ratio	596 bhp per ton
Transmission	Rear drive, 5 speed and reverse, rear-mounted transaxle
Tyre sizes	Front: 500 x 15 / Rear: 650 x 15
Wheelbase	2270 mm (7 ft 5 ins)
Track	Front: 1290 mm (4 ft 3 ins) / Rear: 1260 mm (4 ft 2 ins)
Brakes	Hydraulic disc
Length	3560 mm (11 ft 8 ins)
Width	1490 mm (4 ft 11 ins)
Height	740 mm (2 ft 5 ins)
Weight	427 kg (939 lbs)
Front suspension	Independent, double wishbones, coil spring/damper units
Rear suspension	Independent, top links, radius rods, coil spring/damper units
Top speed	160 mph approx.
0-60 mph	4.5 seconds

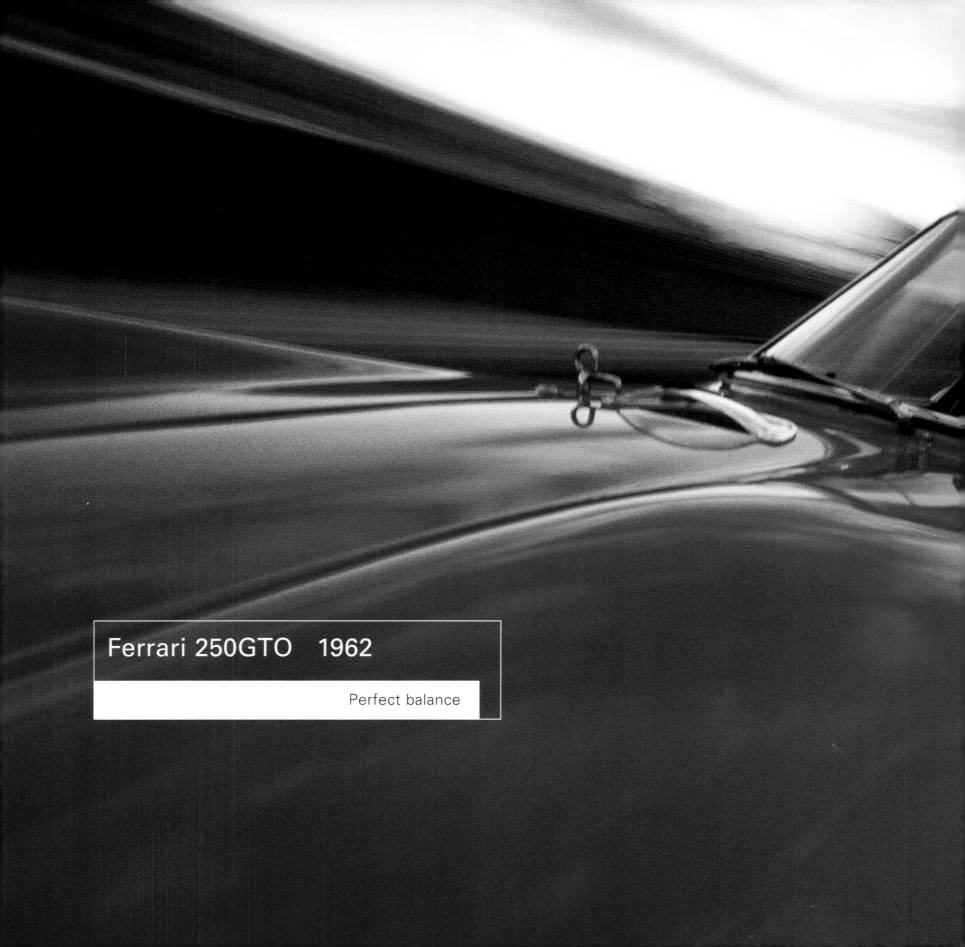

Ferrari 250GTO   1962

Perfect balance

If ever a car looked absolutely right, then it is the Ferrari GT0. The plunging valley between those humpy front wings, the little mouth pouting at the tip of its bonnet, the subtle flip-up on the boot.

Never mind that the nose is long and the tail short and never mind that there are vents and slots and flaps everywhere to break up the sculptured smoothness of the body. The car still looks perfectly balanced in every respect. Prise open the flimsy door with its little handle - which, like most of the minor fittings, looks ready to snap off in the hand rather than trip any mechanism - and slide into the clasp of a welcoming bucket seat whose black leather surface has been polished by nearly 35 years of competition.

Two things immediately demand your attention inside. The gearlever, which sticks up like some mystic sword from a transmission tunnel high enough to rest your elbow, sports a polished aluminium knob the size of a tennis ball. In neutral it lies at exactly the same height as the steering wheel's centre. From its centre, spokes polished bright enough to dazzle support a thin wooden rim and if you simply let go of this and keep the arms bent, your hand falls instantly to the gearknob. It's more than natural. Further down and just to the left of the gate which guides the metal mast beneath your shifting hand, there's a huge speedometer in a plastic-covered cardboard box. Only road legality demands its presence - the all important rev counter with its wide plastic needle and bold but pale white numbers is dead ahead in the main instrument panel.

Already you feel comfortable at the controls, arms and legs bent in best laid-back foetal style, hands on that spindly wheel-rim, legs resting on thoughtfully placed leather-covered pads designed to save the limbs from bruises throughout 24 hours. But now for the noise, which like a signature defines all the cars in this book. First the whirring starter, sounding as if it's turning ten times faster than it is. Then the chuffing and thumping as the cylinders come alive, hissing and spitting back through the 12 carburettor chokes under the bonnet, then booming and drumming round the big silencer boxes further back beneath the seat. The sound is richly textured with a host of extra whistles and whines from a multitude of camshaft drives, pumps and belts. Even when it's fully warmed the GTO's engine never seems really happy at idle or trickling round the paddock. It will, but then you have to give the accelerator a good long prod in order to clear the throat ready for the real performance. Snick the metal ball across and back for first. Feel the subtle mechanical advantage of a long lever and a short shift action, and ease onto the track.

I'm always uneasy about saying I have a favourite car. Rather like the same question about your children, it's far more diplomatic to say they're all important, each in their own special way. However, if I'm forced to commit myself, the 250GTO has more of the qualities that are an essential part of a great car than any other I've come across... probably.

From any aspect the car looks beautiful. Externally it is a gorgeous example of the coachbuilder's art. And when you finally sit in the cockpit, the view over the curved bonnet is still aesthetically pleasing. Turn the engine and the sound matches the view: the classic V-12 configuration and the snap exhausts make all the proper noises.

When you move off there's a nicely matched combination of disc brakes and beautifully balanced suspension with sufficient power to give you the thrill of a competition car without the heart-stopping terror generated by something with 600 bhp. The GTO has a Clark Kent-like capacity to metamorphose into a supercar, but is still well-mannered and forgiving, allowing an amateur driver to get much closer to what a pro driver can achieve with it.

A few yards and the wheel's wooden rim is already telling you things. A ridge in the road from paddock to track, a touch of camber here, a change of surface there. The effort required to steer is minimal, like any modern power-assisted set-up, but there's no such interference here, nothing to mask the feel of the road. No hydraulics or electronics to damp out the little tremors that tell you the surface is broken, or to hide a gentle change of weight which warns of lessening grip. Just pure communication with the tarmac. How did they do it? How could they make steering so light without being twirly and low geared, how could they make it so sharp and accurate without being hard to turn? How delicate it all feels through that varnished brown thin wooden rim when compared with the thick black handful found in today's transport.

Ferrari 250GTO

Now, as the speed picks up, the GTO begins to float rather than drive. Lie back and enjoy the sensation, because there's no effort required. The chassis works in perfect harmony with the steering, as if the whole car is articulating from a point just under your seat. The wheel tells you what to do and you adjust the car's attitude rather than steer it through the corner. It doesn't need to slip its tail or push its nose wide because you felt it coming and made the correction almost before it was necessary. It's like telepathy. If ever there was a car to recapture those glorious 1960s images of Ireland or Moss drifting round Goodwood, the nose of the car angled to the track, but with no steering lock one way or the other, then the GTO is it.

The engine is now well and truly awake, its throat clear and its voice in perfect tune. The downmarket steam engine noises and raggedy beat have been replaced by a rich tenor, swelling from under the bonnet as the revs rise like a chord from a pipe organ. Outside, the four exhaust tailpipes add just a touch of rasping trombone. It's a noise only Ferraris seem able to orchestrate.

A perfect car then... Well, perhaps not quite. A few laps of Silverstone's super smooth and grippy surface make the Ferrari's three-decade-old brakes grumble and grind while the middle pedal edges ever nearer the floor. The gears too will fight back in the face of a hurried shift. The action remains a delight, but timing is essential - too fast and the grating from within jars the palm outstretched round that huge bauble of a gearknob,

In terms of its practicality you can use it on the road, with space to carry a couple of bags, and even in slow-moving traffic the engine doesn't overheat. With all of these qualities the GTO is about as near to perfection as you can get in a single car.

The GTO was the most wanted car on my list. For a long time it could only be an aspiration but there came a point where record royalties meant buying one was a possibility. However rare a car is, there always seem to be one or two for sale at a given moment, and this was one of the best to come up for a considerable time. Most GTOs have an interesting history and a number of successes on their record, but when I bought this car I only knew I had seen it at various Ferrari events, when it stood out because of its condition and the subtle difference of its lines.

The price being asked was significantly more than I expected or was prepared to pay, though with so few 250GTOs in existence - only 39 were built - it was unlikely there would ever be a bargain basement deal. When I saw the car I just thought "yes, yes, yes" and to the amazement of the seller, instead of starting to negotiate, my eyes simply glazed over and I said I'd take it. I think he thought he'd had me over but then he had to sit and watch as its valued soared in the late 1980s, sadly a short-lived phase.

Ferrari 250GTO

With such a build-up, it would not have been a surprise if the car had failed to live up to expectations, but in fact it exceeded them. Over thirty years later it continues to do so, and although I would be pushed to justify it as a practical buy it has given really good service. I've used the car for just about everything, including taking the kids to school in the snow when a modern saloon refused to start. I've raced it in the UK and Europe, competed in various rallies and done thousands of miles just for fun.

I also feel that I have been able to add a little to the GTO's history in the 30-odd years that I've owned it. Thanks to a trend in recent years for two-driver races in GT cars, I can boast that I have shared drives with Stirling Moss, Will Hoy and Justin Bell. There is a lengthy list of great drivers I've been happy to let loose in it - every one of them, if new to the car, has climbed out a convert.

Perhaps the one moment when I knew this was the right car for me was after the deal had been done, when the documents were being handed over. I immediately recognised the original 4HLY registration on the old logbook from a photo I'd taken in 1963 of the car going through the chicane at Goodwood - I'd kept and treasured the photo throughout the years as a reminder of the car I most wanted to own.

too slow and the engine comes jerking up from near idle speed to take up the drive again. Get it right and the flow of acceleration and the seamless step down the musical scale will serenade your success, but it takes practice. And once away from the seductive ergonomics of the GTO's cockpit and the balance of its chassis and steering you realise that the steering is light because the grip from the tyres is fairly low. The tall Dunlops are about the same width as those on an average modern hatchback, but you hadn't noticed because the car's beautiful balance allowed you to carry so much extra speed into and throughout the turns.

The GTO was another favourite amongst these cars, because of its elegant looks and natural cockpit layout, because of its beautiful balance of steering and chassis, and because of the richness of its 12 cylinder soundtrack. It was another fusion of artistry and purpose that progress would sacrifice to the grip of bigger tyres and the downward pressure of aerodynamic development.

The 250GTO evolved from Ferrari's highly successful 250GT series, and consisted of a limited series of 36 cars geared to the Championship of Makes series regulations - hence the 'O' for 'Omologato' (homologated).

This 250GTO, chassis number 3757, was completed in June 1962, and was supplied to the Belgian Ferrari racing team, Ecurie Francorchamps. The car competed at Le Mans in 1962 (as in the poster pictured above), finishing second in class and third overall, driven by Blaton and Dernier, and that same year finished third in both the Coupe du Salon and the Tour de France. The following season it won several major races including the Spa 500 kms (with a new lap record), driven by Willy Mairesse.

Brought to England in 1964, its next owner, Peter Clark, won twice at Oulton Park and achieved a class win at Daytona. After being restored by Bob Houghton in 1977 the car has been in continuous use ever since.

Ferrari 250GTO

Specification	
Engine capacity/configuration	2953 cc/12 cylinders in vee
Valve gear	Single overhead camshaft per bank
Power	296 bhp @ 8000 rpm
Power to weight ratio	288 bhp per ton
Transmission	Rear drive, 5 speed and reverse, synchro gearbox
Tyre sizes	Front: 600 x 15/Rear: 650 x 15
Wheelbase	2400 mm (7 ft 11 ins)
Track	Front: 1351 mm (4 ft 5 ins)/Rear: 1346 mm (4 ft 5 ins)
Brakes	Hydraulic disc
Length	4400 mm (14 ft 5 ins)
Width	1701 mm (5 ft 7 ins)
Height	1245 mm (4 ft 1 in)
Weight	1045 kg (2299 lbs)
Front suspension	Independent, double wishbones, coil springs
Rear suspension	Live axle, radius arms, semi-elliptic springs
Top speed	170 mph
0-60 mph	6.5 seconds

Alfa Romeo TZ   1964

Raucous elegance

The Alfa TZ has not dated like a Ford Anglia or Morris Minor. It still looks fresh and somehow so very Italian, a neat trick that designers from that part of the world seem to manage without apparent effort.

I know too that it is a real purpose-built racing car, made by the Alfa factory and offered as an off-the-shelf racer to anyone with the inclination, and the means. And, as was also typical of Italian cars of the period, the name defines the detail. The 'T' stands for *tubolare* and the 'Z' for Zagato; the first is because the car's frame is formed by a mass of steel tubes like a complicated metal spider's web, and the second because Milanese coachbuilding experts Zagato were the source of that shapely hand-rolled aluminium body.

This last is an item of automotive beauty which seems to melt before your eyes like an ice sculpture, the curves blending effortlessly into one another and for which the sawn-off back end provides not a hasty ending, but a perfect finish. It is a mixture which is both redolent of an era, yet timeless.

Stand back, survey the whole and you have to remind yourself that such a set of curves can form a weapon of battle. The elegant lines and small dimensions make it look somehow too fragile, and boyhood memories of swiftly rusting FIATs and Lancias with electrics that had no clear pattern of operation only add to that impression. But a glance under the one-piece hinge-forward bonnet, the mechanic's delight which exposes all the suspension, engine and cooling in one easy movement, instead reveals the TZ to be massively over-engineered.

My first attempt at buying an Alfa TZ was a startling encounter with Hubris (not the legendary Greek car dealer, but that awful feeling you've been a bit of a mug). I had decided that one of these Alfas was a car I really needed: a lovely little vehicle that was the equivalent of a mini GTO, something all the family would love driving, and still possibly undervalued by the market.

I started work in earnest. I carried out, or so I thought, some extensive research, and found an example with the requisite Le Mans pedigree, a total rebuild I nevertheless thought we could successfully handle inhouse. It belonged to someone I knew well, an American enthusiast with impeccable taste and a fabulous collection of cars.

We had the crates of bits and pieces shipped to England and I proudly announced to the world via the registrar of the Alfa Owners' Club that I had bought this particular car. Someone got in touch rather smartish to say, 'I'm afraid not, son. I've got it.' And he did. It turned out my pretender had been cobbled up from another less interesting Alfa or six.

There are expensive ball joints and adjustable rods throughout the suspension, a hefty steering box and a cat's cradle of idlers and drag links connecting it to the hubs and wheels. Large aluminium structures contain and connect the motive parts and there are yet more castings wherever the fast-breeding economies of mass production would soon require a thin piece of pressed steel. It's no wonder that the Giulia GT volume model, which provided a number of components, cost more than an E-type.

No doubt about it, once you delve beneath its shapely skin the Alfa TZ is built for stamina via the strength of its parts, much like a military vehicle and with a price tag to match. In 1963 you could have bought three competition Lotus Elans for the price of a single TZ, or perhaps more relevant, a reasonable-sized dwelling in the home counties. The TZ was a clean sheet of paper design and bore no resemblance to any Alfa production model, but in 1964 the sum of 3,700,000 Italian lire was a small fortune.

All of which, though, only adds to the sense that even then cars like the TZ were marking the end of an era where large manufacturers were willing to create the means for wealthy amateurs to indulge their passion on the international stage and where the extent and appearance of the engineering they bought mattered as much as its performance. Nevertheless, it was a strategy which had proved effective almost since the dawn of motorised competition. As someone so memorably pointed out, to figure in the results you need to finish the race. Nick's car is a real-world veteran of the 1964 Le Mans 24-Hour race where it finished first in class and eleventh overall driven by Bussinello and Deserti. Eleventh overall... I couldn't help but think about that. That Nick and I might go to France and pit a privately entered 1.6 litre hatchback amongst the current factory-entered Peugeots, Astons and Audis, and expect a result. Different times, of course, because in 1964, you could indeed do exactly that.

Oh, there was a wailing and a gnashing of teeth in the garages of Mason that day, as well as a really horrid dose of shame. I had forgotten, or allowed myself to forget in the excitement of the chase, that there are a significant number of cars around that aren't quite right. And I had underestimated how much money there is to be made in faking those really good cars that fall just below the truly great cars. In one respect I was extremely fortunate that the friend of mine who had sold me the car was not only blameless, but honourable. As soon as he heard the story he took the car back without a quibble, even paying for it to be shipped back to the States.

The quest for another TZ began again, where upon old Hubris had another laugh at my expense. Having gaily suggested in public that the car was one of the most desirable cars in the history of the planet, I had personally helped hike the price up by the time another TZ with Le Mans history came on the market. I am glad to report the credentials of this second car did check out, and no other owners have since emerged from the woodwork to query its authenticity.

Later that year TZ number 11 performed a similar giant-killing feat at the daunting Nürburgring before going to Mexico to do it yet again. Bussinello and Deserti were amateurs in status but clearly experienced behind the wheel, and yet I am sure the crew that tended their TZ never considered the prospect of having to re-engineer anything in order to race. They expected it to work like a road car, and the results say that it did just that. Within three or four years though, the car's international career was over and it was heading for America and comfortable retirement.

Fast forward four decades and historic racing, not to mention purity of line and vintage engineering extravagance, are in fashion once again. The TZ is back in Europe and on track at Anglesey in North Wales where the lines look as fresh and curvaceous as ever, followed by a reminder of their low-line dimensions. There's a double bent, crouching scramble to enter the cramped cockpit and a splay of the knees to clear the steering wheel, a seating position much the same as the hallowed Ferrari GTO's but once in, and despite a need to bend a helmeted head to clear the roof, there's the joy which is just enough room for my legs, even if I'm still not sure I could brake with the side of my foot for my share of 24 hours. Or if I could stand the noise.

The lightly-modified 1600 cc engine that started life in the Giulia saloon is shapely like the body which covers it, but it makes a noise entirely out of proportion to its dimensions. What's more, it bellows forth via an exhaust pipe that exits in the middle of the car and on the left, just below the driver's door. Fussy and fractious at lower revs, hunting and barking as if it's about to run out of fuel, then as the engine climbs up the scale, clears its throat with a mighty rasp that is both hoarse and booming at the same time. A bottom of the barrel intensity that makes earplugs an absolute must.

And yet, within a few tours of Anglesey's picturesque coastal track, I have forgotten about the noise, the constant rattle of helmet against roofline, the angle of my foot and the fact that my knee hits the gearlever and knocks it out of second. All these things I overlook, seduced by a drive that is as intimate as the lines are attractive. The car talks to me, lets me know when it's happy with the way I handle it, and more important, when it's not. Warns that I have overstepped the mark and if I carry on pushing the accelerator it will have no option but to react and sling its tail. And because it keeps me so well informed, I soon decide to work with the car rather than against it. I try and carry a bit more momentum on the way into the corners rather than out of them.

I try and brake a little less hard for the fast ones and carry in more speed but not so much that the front end gives up before I get to the apex. Press a middle pedal which is firmer and less tactile than some, hear the rear tyres start to whimper, keep the steering straight lest they lift off and lock up, then gently ease towards the corner. As long as I keep it all tidy and measured, I have to push very hard indeed to turn a gentle nosing wide into anything more challenging, but when I finally do reach the limit, pulling in a mild dose of loose tail is more about unravelling the two thirds of a turn or so of lock than winding on a great armful of opposite. It's easy but oddly inert, as if there's a load of play somewhere in those links and boxes way down in that elegant nose. I learn too, to manage the long

This car lived up to all my expectations. It looks absolutely gorgeous, a miniature of those extremely elegant lines that embody great Italian design, and drives beautifully, with that balance of chassis, brakes and engine that makes older cars so enjoyable.

Desperate to attend the Goodwood Revival with this new gem, I took the car even though it was not entirely ready to go. With an insouciant wave I assured my trusty crew that as the engine had just been done we could reliably enter the car. I was going to drive the Alfa with the legendary Bobby Rahal. In qualifying Bobby immediately proved unbelievably quick. He was recording times matching those I'd done the year before in the GTO, and this car had an engine half the size.

Bobby said he had 'often admired the TZ from afar, but it wasn't until I actually had the pleasure of driving Nick's car that I truly understood what made the TZ such a great race car. While not blessed with tremendous power the superb balance between braking and handling, its nimbleness in changing direction and the overwhelming sense of confidence I received through the entire car allowed me as a driver

Alfa Romeo TZ

to continue to push it to the limit – knowing full well that when I found it, the car would give me all the signs I needed to ensure I understood that I was there.'

Sadly, come the race, Bobby managed only one lap before an elderly driveshaft resigned. The engine was clearly working too well, and we now had a shaft shaped more like a CurlyWurly, and more importantly no longer attached to any drive train. I have preserved the driveshaft's remains as the memento of yet another lesson to be learnt.

gearlever for the five-speed gearbox which lies almost horizontal and which moves up and down rather than forward and back. It must be guided rather than grasped and I soon remember that as long as I aim the lever in a general direction but keep the fingers loose, the box will find the right ratio.

It soon becomes an essential tool to keep the raucous little twin overhead cam engine in its happy phase between 5,500 and 7,500 rpm. Helps maintain the assault on the eardrums. If I don't, the engine falls off a shelf below 5,000 and lapses into a sulky stutter. Once I accept that bullying the car round the track doesn't make it go any faster but involves a load of risk and sweat for no benefit, the Alfa is very easy to drive, and very satisfying. I don't have that nagging feeling that I could go so much faster if only I could understand the car. Stamina is clearly the best basis for success.

By the end of the day, the Alfa feels ever more like the honest hard-working companion it was all those years ago and with the added sense that it was created by a large organisation whose style of engineering and presentation was part of its heritage and needed to be upheld. Even in 1963 the TZ was a little like the handsome actor still doing action movies at the age of 50. Still capable of doing the job in a style which is all his own and with the added bonus of great conversation and old-fashioned manners.

The Alfa Romeo Giulia Tubolare Zagato, to give the car its full title, was first manufactured in 1963, replacing the Giulietta SZ – Sprint Zagato – model. Alfa sub-contracted development to Autodelta SpA, a new specialist tuning and development company set up by Alfa-trained former Ferrari chief engineer Ing. Carlo Chiti and his partner Ludovico Chizzola. The new TZ was a purpose-built GT racing car, based upon an ultra-lightweight, welded-tube (tubolare in Italian) spaceframe chassis.

Milan coachbuilders Carrozzeria Zagato adopted Dr Wunibald Kamm's aerodynamic theories for the TZ's distinctive rear-end treatment, the coda tronca, or 'short tail', which had been tried out to good effect on the Sprint Zagato cars. The new TZ burst onto the racing scene at the 1963 FISA Monza Cup, taking the first four places in the prototype category.

This particular car – chassis number 750 011 – was registered in April 1964 and started its racing career on a high in that summer's Le Mans 24-Hour Race. Driven by Roberto Bussinello and Bruno Deserti it won its class, and placed 11th overall. The following two years then saw it contest the Coppa Città di Enna driven by Guido Rava while leading works driver Jean Rolland ran it at the Chamrousse and Mont-Dore hill climbs.

In 1965 Alfa Romeo released a handful of much-improved, low-line, TZ variants, known as the TZ2, the original model sometimes being referred to, retrospectively, as the TZ1.

Alfa Romeo TZ

Specification	
Engine capacity / configuration	1570 cc/4 cylinders inline
Valve gear	Twin overhead camshafts
Power	155 bhp @ 8000 rpm
Power to weight ratio	246 bhp per ton
Transmission	Rear drive, 5 speed and reverse, synchromesh
Tyre sizes	Front: 500 x 15/Rear: 550 x 15
Wheelbase	2200 mm (7 ft 3 ins)
Track	Front: 1300 mm (4 ft 3 ins)/Rear: 1330 mm (4 ft 4 ins)
Brakes	Hydraulic disc
Length	3950 mm (13 ft)
Width	1510 mm (4 ft 11 ins)
Height	1200 mm (3 ft 11 ins)
Weight	650 kg (1433 lbs)
Front suspension	Independent, wishbones, coil springs
Rear suspension	Independent, lower wishbones, coil springs
Top speed	157 mph
0-60 mph	7.5 seconds

Ferrari 512S   1970

The art of noise

How could an engine make so much noise? I sat in the local hostelry the evening after my time in the Ferrari 512S, listening to the waterfall in my left ear and hoping the inability to hear anything less than a shout might only be temporary.

I wondered too about the effect it must have had on the drivers of the day. I had the luxury of modern earplugs, but like fireproof overalls and full-face helmets, these were items unknown to Nino Vaccarella or the Rodriguez brothers. How on earth they stood it for 24 hours I simply cannot imagine.

The sheer intensity of the cacophony once the engine is running seems all at odds with the delicate precision of the 512's cockpit layout. It was sufficiently small that my helmeted head just poked out of the open roof but gave enough room below for legs, elbows and feet to be comfortable in the job. There was also that primeval cocoon feeling that I had experienced in the D-Type, again because all the cockpit's edges curve round you. Added to which the Ferrari's screen is so deep and so rounded it might have been cut from a glass sphere. I felt for all the world as if I were sitting in some automotive goldfish bowl.

Great stalky legs sprouting from the tops of the front wings are needed to bring the tiny rear view mirrors up to eye level and the screen's bottom edge swoops down to meet a dashboard so low it seems to lie just above your outstretched knees. And that miniature rev counter stage centre in front of you surely cannot be large enough to report revolutions from something so loud. But then equally certain is that the tiny three-spoked steering wheel cannot be enough to control the beast that is about to be uncaged.

The huge sound begins with a whirr from the starter, soon drowned by a metallic thrashing like a pound of bolts tumbling in a spin drier. The long train of gears taking drive from the crankshaft to each of the four camshafts is only inches behind my head and a hundred harmonics clatter up and down as the shocks from opening and shutting 24 valves explores the backlash in a thousand sets of teeth. Rev it a little. Amazingly, the exhaust and inlet noise is able to rise above the gnashing, but only just. 3,000 and the note begins to harden. At exactly five it turns to a howl, as if someone has pressed a different key on a board. You can sit there and gently float the engine's revs between four-eight and five-two and it's as if that same person is trilling the keys. Ferraris do this kind of thing. There's always something, some individual signature, some particular theme in the noise that beckons you. Uncanny, but seductive.

Once secure in that glorious bowl of a cockpit there's the customary fumble with the Ferrari gearshift gate to find first gear and the promise of more fumbling if you don't follow the prescribed sequence and go all the way up or down through the box. Signor Ferrari obviously didn't want his drivers to stray from the norm and miss out any ratios on the way. And then you drive off.

I must have been suffering from a nasty bout of overconfidence to think I really needed this car. If I'd paused to think for a while I would have realised the only drivers who'd achieved success in the car were amongst the greatest of all time (and some of those are no longer with us). The 512S came with a reputation as a truly fearsome beast, from a era of the fastest Le Mans races of all time.

This particular car's pedigree was high-class. It was originally a team car for the 1970 season: Mario Andretti had had a win in the States, and Ronnie Peterson and Derek Bell drove it at Le Mans, where it had been involved in a crash. The following year it was used in the filming of the Steve McQueen movie 'Le Mans'. During one of the stunts a dramatic cockpit fire got out of control and guaranteed the familiar scenario of the entire car turning up in pieces.

It had been languishing in a Parisian warehouse through the 1970s until the film production company had a clear-out. I'm still embarrassed that, despite the fact I picked it up quite cheaply for around £6000, I wrote and asked for some money back because a part was missing. The sellers quite rightly did not bother replying.

After some initial work at Greypaul Motors, the rebuild was completed at Rosso Racing, which Bob Houghton had set up with Vic Norman, an old friend of mine whose catchphrase "It's not dear" has been responsible for me making a number of major investments in technical toys. The reconstruction was complicated by the built-in obsolescence of components for racing cars: castings made using magnesium rather than aluminium are lighter, but tend to disintegrate to powder within a few years. This car was already eight or nine years old by the time I acquired it, and some components were missing or had been damaged in the fire.

Vic and I went on a pilgrimage to Switzerland to see Herbie Muller, a well-known sports car driver who knew as much as anyone about these cars, and had an Aladdin's cave of old 512 parts. The only problem was that although many were brand new, they were already passing their expiry date. Nonetheless we still found a considerable, and expensive, quantity of parts, shovelled them into the boot and hurried back. Sadly I had the misfortune to be driving in the last 1000km sports car race at the Nürburgring in 1981 when Herbie, a great driver and genuinely nice man, died in an accident.

The rebuild of the 512S took three years, most of the time being spent in the making or tracking down of components for these unique cars. All too often the excitement of sourcing an apparently identical part would turn to gloom as it transpired that it was from an M type rather than S and would not fit. Although I

Just like that. There is no monster lurking within to suddenly administer any savage assault. The 512 just sweeps effortlessly away down the straight, that searing, screeching engine delivering huge amounts of smooth and progressive power from the very bottom of that tiny tacho's scale all the way to the top. It is such a contrast to the turbocharged explosion of the F40 and so unlike the promise when I first started the engine. Even the gears seemed to find their way in without quite the fiddle I was expecting.

As I settled in, and started to push harder, the Ferrari seemed to leave its clamour behind and set about gobbling up the circuit in earnest. A gentle push at the front end slowly faded as the slower corners unwound, the motion moving back along the chassis until the tail gently yawed on the exit, pushed wide by the vast punch from that 12 cylinder engine. The 512S didn't affect the lazy sweep through the corners of its 512 BB descendant, and didn't have the pin-sharp bite of the little Lola. Neither did it feature great wings to push it down to the track. The 512S instead had a little of each while always maintaining a superb balance. Neither end of the car showed great strength or weakness, each always complementing the other, and because the suspension was supple without being sloppy, the body was always under control while giving accurate information as to what had disturbed it. It was always possible to feel what was happening and be ready to react in plenty of time.

This composure meant that the 512S didn't feel shatteringly fast and yet it was comfortably quicker round the lap than both the 512 BB of 1979, and the F40 which came 10 years after that. True, some of this was down to the enormously strong engine but perhaps the seamless way the power poured from it with no sudden rushes or surges made it seem less so. And certainly anything that is capable of lapping that quickly would have a dark side when handled sufficiently badly - maybe this is the subtle difference between a car built officially to defend Ferrari's fortunes and to be crewed by the world's best, and those like the 512 BB that were built for sale to allcomers. Whatever, of the sports cars in this book, the 512S was only shaded on lap times by the two Porsches. Quite easily by the 962 thanks to its huge weight of downforce but only just by the 935, despite its enormous turbo power.

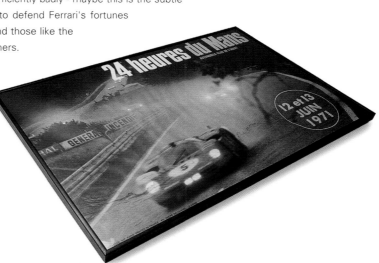

119

Ferrari 512S

was impatient to drive the car, one of the greatest pleasures of a rebuild is the chance to loiter round the workshops. Additionally I had learnt from running my own garage business that the impending visit of a customer will frequently upgrade the work from pending to action.

Generally I believe cars should be restored as closely as possible to their original state, or as they ran in their prime. In this instance I made an exception and decided to opt for the body configuration of the Spider version, with a short tail and open cockpit. Visibility on the Le Mans versions was limited, and it's noticeable on photos of the cars how many different attempts are made to provide some kind of rear vision: mirrors on struts, mirrors on the roof. They're not just for the vanity of the driver, honestly.

The fact is that with the intense vibrations and enormous waves of body and wings, it's almost impossible to see anything behind you, and maybe the Ferrari works drivers arrogantly assumed there was little need since no one would overtake them. For the kind of club racing I was anticipating, going for an open cockpit and better vision seemed less claustrophobic and much more practical.

By the time the 512S was ready for racing I had moved onto modern sports cars, but this did not stop me from, rather unchivalrously, running the car for its debut in a Ferrari-only race at Donington. Since the closest competitor was a mildly modified road-going Boxer, I do remember the marshal offering odds on whether I would be able to lap the entire field by the end of the race.

If this all sounds too perfect, then so be it. The 512S simply felt so right and was so much more accurate and more precise than its two successors. It needed a firm hand but that was easy to administer because it always gave you plenty of warning and didn't spring any surprises.

I even came to like the noise, like a favourite anthem played far too loud. That and the hugely muscular engine that made the sound, the chassis balance that let you cope with it all from that glassy cockpit with its glorious sensation of the world flashing past. All of these contained within that purposeful ground-hugging shape, made the 512S especially memorable. I even forgot about the long brake pedal and sticky gearshift.

The 512S was built by Ferrari in 1970, the design a direct result of the decision that sports cars would be limited to five litres from 1968. To qualify for this limit it was stipulated that 25 examples would have to be built. Porsche had taken full advantage of this with the 917, and now Fiat backed Ferrari to build a competitor - the 512S.

This particular car - chassis number 1026 - was run as a works team car, competing in the 1970 24-hour Daytona, where it came third, driven by Andretti, Merzario and Ickx. A first place at the 12-hour Sebring race was followed by a fourth in the 1000kms at Monza, but at Le Mans that year the car, driven by Bell and Peterson, was  *withdrawn after four hours. Following the race the car was used in the movie 'Le Mans'. After a special effects fire the car was stored for eight years in Paris. Since restoration it has been regularly raced and demonstrated.*

Ferrari 512S

Specification	
Engine capacity / configuration	4993 cc / 12 cylinders in vee
Valve gear	Twin overhead camshafts per bank
Power	550 bhp @ 8500 rpm
Power to weight ratio	666 bhp per ton
Transmission	Rear drive, 5 speed and reverse, syncromesh transaxle
Tyre sizes	Front:110 / 235 x 15 / Rear: 150/260 x 15
Wheelbase	2400 mm (7 ft 11 ins)
Track	Front: 1518 mm (5 ft 0 ins) / Rear: 1511 mm (5 ft 0 ins)
Brakes	Hydraulic disc
Length	4140 mm (13 ft 7 ins)
Width	1955 mm (6 ft 5 ins)
Height	990 mm (3 ft 3 ins)
Weight	840 kg (1848 lbs)
Front suspension	Independent, double wishbones, coil spring / dampers
Rear suspension	Independent, lwr wishbone, top links, radius arms, coil spring / dampers
Top speed	195mph
0-60 mph	3.3 seconds

Ferrari 356 GTB/4 Daytona   1972

The price of progress

Ferrari 356 GTB/4 Daytona

That Daytona is so ugly, someone said, it might not even be a Ferrari. It was that same person, though, who only a day later remarked how good it looked through the camera lens.

I admit I had the same feeling about the driving experience. At first the Daytona felt so heavy, uncomfortable and remote after the light and elegant GTO and although the chuffing and hissing rhythm section was pumping away from the moment you pressed the starter, as was the 12 cylinder smoothness and Ferrari howl once you got moving, it was nowhere near so involving. Right from the start, you didn't feel so close to the action. On the move, the Daytona's steering had a low-geared spongy feel, not that much heavier to turn but nothing like as communicative. And where the GTO had floated round the track seemingly without contact with the road, the Daytona jarred and jiggled over every ridge and crevice. It wasn't as friendly, either. Brake just a touch too late or fail to catch the tail in its first ten degrees of yaw and you were in trouble.

A few laps, however, and the Daytona's driving experience did begin to grow on me. Bigger tyres generate more grip and suspension has to be stiffer to cope. More weight needs more power to move it. The Daytona showed the nature of a decade's progress and no matter how much you might mourn the passing of such as the GTO, the Daytona began to feel more familiar to someone brought up on more modern machinery. The lap times inevitably were faster than the GTO's, but equally inevitable was that the artistry of the four-wheel drift was impossible; there was no place for anything in the Daytona's manual but the dedication to maximum grip. Ten years on from the GTO, it was the start of the 1970s. This was the beginning of the modern era.

From the outside, the Daytona even looks half as heavy again as its predecessor, an impression heightened by its broad flat bonnet and minimal distance between rear wheels and upright boot. Inside, it immediately feels more like the road car from which it was developed. The relationship between seat and steering is less accommodating, and although the wheel still has polished spokes, the rim is leather-covered and is distant and tilted forward from the vertical. You sit on rather than in the seat which leans back at a reclining angle and is covered with that strange bath towel material found on Italian cars of the period. In this case it's blue, which clashes with the red seat belts that slip off the shoulders all too easily. Move the seat to outstretch the legs and you can't reach the wheel. Do the opposite and your legs are splayed and your feet are angled. How they drove this for 24 hours I don't know, or, more to the point, if they could make the GTO fit all sizes, why not this.

The Daytona is a perfect example of my inability to part with cars I like. I have owned three and only managed to dispose of one; my justification has been that the differences between them, though subtle, are sufficient to require a brace.

I first bought a Daytona in 1977, choosing a left-hand drive version because I thought the Continent was the only place I could use it to the full outside the constraints of British roads and the eagle-eyed traffic police. Curiously enough I found myself not long afterwards spending six months recording in the south of France, with endless opportunities to gain enormous appreciation of the car as one of the great road-going Ferraris, as well as an intimate knowledge of the exorbitant cost of tyres in the Alpes-Maritimes.

By Ferrari standards it's a large car - some people call it a truck, and you certainly wouldn't want to try and park it in Monaco - but once you're inside, it's an extremely comfortable cockpit with plenty of room. This is certainly true in comparison with the next generation of rear-engined cars, in particular the Boxer, where there's barely space for the most fitted of luggage, let alone my preferred personal paraphernalia of maps, old apple cores, souvenirs and unusual French sausages.

Under the guise of a spring-clean, I assembled a number of my road cars and exchanged them for something I thought would be far more impractical in the shape of an early competition Daytona, but with its lightweight body and uprated engine that car in fact turned out to be an even nicer road car than the standard version.

So when a dealer rang to offer me this once-in-a-lifetime opportunity I was irresistibly lured by the fact that its giant fuel tank made the boot unusable, its plastic windows were no substitute for air-conditioning, the side exhausts were bordering on the illegal and the huge wheel-arch flares (bordering on bell bottoms) covered competition wheels and tyres unavailable from any regular retailer. To top it all, this particular cake was iced not only in bright Ecurie Francorchamps yellow, but with a Le Mans finish.

The transmission tunnel is lower than the 250's and the gearlever is shorter and further away to the right, topped with a common old round black plastic knob. The speedo and rev counter are in the normal place in the panel ahead of you and you look down at this cockpit instead of becoming an intimate part of it. Every-

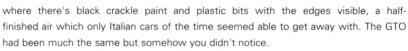

where there's black crackle paint and plastic bits with the edges visible, a half-finished air which only Italian cars of the time seemed able to get away with. The GTO had been much the same but somehow you didn't notice.

The noise of the engine starting was either more refined or more remote depending on your point of view, but it was still all Ferrari, and it did sound more powerful as befits its extra 1.4 litres and 100 horsepower. Not louder, but more intense and with a smoothness you could hear but not feel. Easing out on to the track, feeling every bump on the way out of the paddock and listening to the clonks and grunts from the differential in the rear axle as it sorts out the balance of power against grip, the Daytona feels ready for the battle which would surely inhibit the GTO's artistic display.

Build up the speed and the steering's weight becomes more noticeable, although the springy, spongy feel that I felt in the paddock has been replaced with a strong self-centring action and the car's blunt nose will point into the corners with a precision I had not expected. Through the turn, and with that silky power pouring forth, the Daytona nears its limit in a series of little twitches rather than a smooth slide, either pointing its nose or tail. Either needs swift attention and there's no feeling that the car is with you - you need to drive it all the time. Show it a firm hand and you can appreciate its strengths, relax and it will fight back. The brakes, meanwhile, grumbled, groaned and rattled through the body and steering wheel - just like the GTO's - although the pedal stayed firmer for longer. The more distant gearchange, which hadn't promised such easy access, did in fact shift the gears that much better. The short lever slipped into the slotted gate more easily. Moving it faster didn't elicit a crunch, it just changed the gears more quickly.

But with each shift, you didn't feel as if you were taking hold of something which stirred the mechanicals at the very heart of the car like you did in the GTO. Now you were operating a piece of machinery. Still with a feel unique to Ferrari, with that strange sensation that each thrust into the slotted metal gate was like chopping a piece of hard rubber with a sharp knife, you would grudgingly have to admit that progress had made the task of shifting gears more efficient.

The Daytona is a road car adapted for racing and it shows. It had adopted the attitude of making everything bigger so it won't break rather than making it more efficient to lessen the stress. It required a firm grasp at all times, but the more you drove it, the better you managed its mass, the more it seemed to stop twitching and sweep through the corners. Ten years on, an extra 100 horsepower and three or four inches on the tyres had only brought a one and a half second improvement in lap times, and at the cost of so much pleasure. What price progress.

There were only 15 'Competizione' 365 GTB/4s made across three series - 16 including the sole aluminium-bodied car built in 1969. The Daytona name was Ferrari's internal designation for the prototype. This was in honour of the company's triumph at Daytona in 1967, when they humbled the Ford GT40s on their home soil, finishing first, second and third with two 330 P4s and a P3. However, the name leaked out and although Ferrari immediately dropped it, the nickname stuck thereafter.

This car, chassis number 15373, came from the second series of competition cars produced, and was built by the factory for Jacques Swaters' Ecurie Francorchamps team, who ran this car at Le Mans in 1972, where it was co-driven by Derek Bell, Teddy Pilette and Richard Bond (picture above). They finished fourth in class and eighth overall. The car was then owned for some time by Bob Roberts, owner of the Midland Motor Museum. It was briefly re-painted black in the belief that this would make it less conspicuous to the local constabulary.

Ferrari 356 GTB/4 Daytona

Specification

Engine capacity/configuration	4390 cc/12 cylinders in vee
Valve gear	Twin overhead camshafts per bank
Power	405 bhp @ 8300 rpm
Power to weight ratio	358 bhp per ton
Transmission	Rear drive, 5 speed and reverse, synchromesh, rear-mounted transaxle
Tyre sizes	Front 215/700 x 15/Rear: 225/700 x 15
Wheelbase	2400 mm (7 ft 11 ins)
Track	Front: 1490 mm (4 ft 11 ins)/Rear: 1475 mm (4 ft 10 ins)
Brakes	Hydraulic, disc and servo assistance
Length	4395 mm (14 ft 5 ins)
Width	1843 mm (6 ft 1 in)
Height	1220 mm (4 ft 0 in)
Weight	1454 kg (3199 lbs)
Front suspension	Independent, unequal length wishbones, coil spring/damper units
Rear suspension	Independent, unequal length wishbones, coil spring/damper units
Top speed	180 mph+
0-60 mph	5.4 secs

Porsche 935 K3   1978

Brute purpose

Porsche 935 K3

There was a school of engineering thought that said "If you make things bigger, they won't break".

The long-tailed Porsche 935 is a bit more sophisticated than that, but at first it's hard to see where. It has a huge square clutch pedal that needs the muscles of Garth to depress and which pulls a large steel hawser along the floor beneath your seat. The gearlever is suitably huge to match, like a refugee from some Peterbilt or Foden and forming the summit of a metal tower sprouting from the floor. Then you discover there are only four speeds in the gearbox. Fire up the flat six engine which hangs out way behind and it sounds as if it has a serious problem. Hunting and surging, burping and spluttering. You can almost hear great bucketfuls of fuel cascading down into its horizontal cylinders. Hold the foot constant on the throttle and it takes fully five seconds to clear its throat. Then, amazingly, it will run smoothly.

All of this is nothing compared with the driving experience. The simple task of driving round the paddock and out on to the circuit is a series of lunges and bunny hops. Wind on full lock and the car grinds to a halt as if you have run up against a kerb. A bit more boot, clear out the engine and flex the leg muscles to slip the clutch and the whole lot unwinds, the rear wheels juddering in a kind of corkscrew motion. Then it all winds up again and needs another load of boot, so you sort of walk the car round the turn, rear wheels scrabbling and scratching at the paddock's broken surface.

Not, you would think, a recipe for success at that most stressful of all races, the Le Mans 24 hours. As it turns out, though, the car's initially unfriendly demeanour is symptomatic of several defence mechanisms against the rigours of that race, and also perhaps the inherent shortcomings of the Porsche's rear-engined layout. But first, the engine. It is air-cooled so there is no potential for damage from coolant leaks or stones through the radiator, and it is massively, hugely powerful. Two big turbochargers are lazy when called upon to spin up and deliver boost, but make up for that with huge volumes of air. This needs massive amounts of fuel to match - both to liberate power and to keep the engine's cylinders cool internally - but because this was in the days before electronic control of fuel injection, the mechanical variety is miles too rich on tickover. Hence the lumpy, grumpy idle.

Secondly, the four speed gearbox. Transmission breakage is probably still the most common reason for retirement at Le Mans, so if you have fewer gears, the drivers have less opportunity to break them. The teeth can also be wider because there is more space in the cluster. Then, if you eliminate the differential altogether and join the rear wheels together by a solid shaft, out goes another fragile item, added to which, it almost eliminates wheelspin.

The Le Mans race of 1979, when I competed in the Lola T297, was my first visit: I'd never been as a spectator and maybe I thought driving was a good way of saving the entrance fee. From the cockpit of my car I could observe this particular Porsche rushing up in my mirrors and passing me on a frighteningly regular basis.

The same thing happened in 1980, when added interest was provided by Paul Newman being part of the 935 squad that finished second, and I was only saved from further embarrassment the following year thanks to a prior engagement at Earl's Court - in that race this car came fourth overall and finished first in class. It was a period when Porsche were so successful with the 935s at Le Mans that the number of entries they were allowed was restricted to prevent the race turning into the Porsche Challenge Cup.

The fact that the 935 had been an important part of Le Mans history for the best part of a decade, rather than one freak year, was particularly appealing. I had been toying with the idea of buying one for some time, and was looking for that window that sometimes exists between the end of a car's useful racing life and before it

But surely, if this was how to succed at Le Mans, why did everybody else bother with the complexity of things Porsche did without? The answer is simply that nobody else had such a powerful yet reliable turbo engine and nobody else chose to hang it out the back where it can swing like a pendulum. Let me explain with a lap of Silverstone's South circuit.

Hop, grunt, scrabble, lump, lump, burp, bruurp to get out of the paddock, then stagger away towards the first corner, slipping the clutch like crazy to stop the engine bogging down. Once fully connected, first gear is good for 90mph, but you can now see why the clutch needs such a heavy foot. The gearshift then snicks the next three gears as fast as you can move the lever despite its lorry-like appearance. Second brings only a minimal drop in revs, and third feels nearly as close but there's a big wait for boost to arrive. When it does, the wallop is vast. Not a sudden explosion like the F40's, but more like a rumbling volcano. Unstoppable once it gets there but giving the tyres more chance to cope with 750 horsepower.

becomes a sought-after collectable. Many of the 935s in America were expensive and had been altered for new formulas, but this car - which I was all too familiar with - had been continuously raced since its Le Mans days in almost its original form.

With such a lengthy competition history and the Porsche factory's efficiency, parts for these cars are rarely a problem, except to the chequebook. Our most serious problem was that the original wheels had been made to accept a now obsolete Dunlop DeNovo tyre, so we had to go to some lengths to modify them.

In no time, this hugely long-tailed, ultimate 911 is travelling at 170 mph and still pulling hard in its fourth and final gear, engine now clear and sweet and putting out the noise that only an air-cooled flat six in the back of a Porsche can make. A hoarse-throated braying from the exhaust trailing behind all the mechanical thrashings and groanings from the engine, like a sort of deranged donkey in concert with a jet engine and a spin drier. Up front, the nose has a slightly darty feel, suggesting it is ready to go where you point it, despite the 911's unique corner-to-corner rock and roll as the weight of the engine dips the tail and picks up the nose. As it does, the wheel fidgets and kicks in your hands and makes you feel in touch with the road.

This is a car that just gets up and goes... and goes and goes. As soon as you climb in it you can imagine charging off down the straight at Le Mans. It's just a shame about the corners, where even the little Lola could get close enough to experience the heat from the gouts of flame coming out of the exhaust pipes as the throttle was shut off. The 935 has sometimes been called a triumph of engineering over design, but for me the form perfectly illustrates the function - brutal, ferocious and determined to crush the opposition.

Hit the brakes. These are another Porsche strong point - the 911's pedal is firm and consistent and the bite at the discs reassuring and strong. Ease the wheel right for Stowe and the darty steering initially noses the car towards the apex, then loses some of its authority. More lock restores it, but it feels awkward, as if a rear end which is half as wide again wants to roll round a curve twice the radius needed by a narrow, dainty nose. Meanwhile I had planted the throttle in a late attempt to elbow the tail round and help the turn. Boost arrived and with it a vast surge of power, but instead of helping, the nose headed straight stage left as if the front tyres had hit a wet patch on the track. The road was fast disappearing so I backed off and the front promptly went through the same dart-then-wait litany as it had at the beginning. The corner meanwhile was a lost cause.

The solid axle between the rear wheels is designed in part to harness huge horse-power by uniting the two tyres, but it was also contributing enormously to the push at the front end. Surely this was a handicap too large to be overcome by sheer power and mechanical stamina. Surely the front tyres would cook before even ten laps were done let alone an hour and a half's stint. A pause for thought and a change of technique perhaps.

One of the 911's more normal problems is a willingness to swing its tail if you carry a touch too much speed into a corner - not an obvious handicap here thanks mainly to the axle - but maybe I could summon it back to assist my cornering efforts. I tried deliberately getting in too fast while still trailing the brakes, then booting it and hoping the boost would arrive just as the tail swung. Hopefully, the push at the front would cancel the swing at the back and we would race round the corner. It was only partially successful because the tail proved amazingly hard to provoke, but it did suggest that a deep entry to the turn was best, getting the car pointing straight as soon as possible before launching it along the shallowest radius available. Then, just occasionally there would be the slightest of twitches from those huge rear tyres, but it was a rare event.

For all this, though, the car was quick round the lap. Quicker for instance than the little Lola or the magnificent 512S Ferrari although it felt nothing like as fast. You could argue that so it should be with all that power and those massive tyres, but it was nevertheless an interesting machine. Built for one purpose only, to survive at Le Mans, it was a unique set of compromises - some inherent in the original design, some deliberately introduced for the task in hand. It was a hugely specialised, ultimate variation of an already quirky road car. We will probably never see its like again.

The 935 was effectively a 911 body shell, adapted to comply with the new regulations, which Porsche interpreted as liberally as possible, for example retaining the rear window as required, but constructing a totally new, more streamlined window over the existing one.

This car, chassis number 930 890 0022, was supplied by Porsche to the Kremer team, who modified it and gave it the K3 suffix. Kremer then ran it in the 1978 and 1979 Le Mans events with Gurdjian, Schornstein and Winter driving in 1978; and Plankenhorn, Schornstein and Winter in 1979.

However its best result at Le Mans came after being purchased by Dudley Wood and privately entered for the 1980 and 1981 races - in 1981 being driven to fourth place overall and first in class by Wood with John Cooper and Claude Bourgoignie. In the mid-80s, the car competed successfully in the UK Thunder-sports Championship.

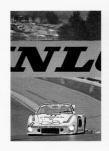

Porsche 935 K3

Specification	
Engine capacity/configuration	3211 cc twin turbo chargers/6 opposed cylinders
Valve gear	Double overhead camshafts per bank
Power	750 bhp @ 8200 rpm
Power to weight ratio	786 bhp per ton
Transmission	Rear drive, 4 speed and reverse, mid-mounted synchromesh transaxle
Tyre sizes	Front: 280/610 R x 16/Rear: 325/650 R x 18
Wheelbase	2225 mm (7 ft 4 ins)
Track	Front: 1445 mm (4 ft 9 ins)/Rear: 1630 mm (5 ft 4 ins)
Brakes	Hydraulic disc
Length	4820 mm (15 ft 10 ins)
Width	1985 mm (6 ft 6 ins)
Height	1150 mm (3 ft 9 ins)
Weight	970 kg (2134 lbs)
Front suspension	Independent, MacPherson struts, lower wishbones
Rear suspension	Live axle, semi-trailing arms, coil spring/damper units
Top speed	203 mph
0-60 mph	5.9 secs

Ferrari 312T3   1978

In the master's chair

Nick has talked much about the drivers he admires because they were important parts of the motivation to purchase. My job has been to take you for the ride. If though, I am allowed to name just one personal hero, it would be Gilles Villeneuve.

The little French-Canadian was neither the best nor the most successful, but he was always going for it. Forever on that knife edge between success and oblivion, whenever he was on track you waited for the inevitable proof of his uncanny skill. For him, no skid was ever irretrievable and to see him drive was to watch a man possessed of such belief in his car control that it was almost palpable. Tragically it was a faith so complete that it left no room for freak circumstance, and it cost him his life.

To sit in the car with which he won his first Grand Prix was thus a special pleasure, the more so because Ferrari 312T3 number 34 is the only Formula 1 Ferrari among these cars. Just study its proportions for a moment. The foreshortened, chunky appearance which contrasts oddly with the triangulated wings; narrow and deep at the rear, wide and shallow at the front. The 312 looked different then and still does to this day. Look a little closer and see that all the major components are made by Ferrari. The car, the engine and the gearbox. Always has been and, we must hope, always will be. No question of using a Hewland or a Cosworth from someone else's factory. No question, either, of doing it the easy way.

Formula 1 Ferraris of this age had to have 12 cylinders. But 12 cylinders makes for a long engine and, because they are laid flat, it is also wide. Ferrari's answer was to make the sidepods big enough to cover the engine but use them to house radiators and coolers. In order to keep the wheelbase short behind the long engine, they turned the gearbox sideways like a modern saloon car's. This is the 'T' in 312T3, standing for 'trasversale'. The shift to operate this has another Ferrari essential, a gate which guides the lever. Where Brabham or Lotus or Tyrrell decided that the direction already provided by their off-the-shelf Hewland transmissions was enough, Ferrari provided not only a slotted gate, but a sequential lock. By making the driver go up or down through all the gears in sequence, Ferrari hoped to avoid a wrong one which might over-rev a precious flat 12 engine. It was like the one fitted to the 512S sports car and, as I would soon find out, much more annoying.

This car has had a traumatic life, but against the odds, has come out on top courtesy of a little help from its friends at Ferrari. I'd originally been charmed by the T3's connection with Gilles Villeneuve. He had won his home Canadian Grand Prix in 1978 in this car - and if I needed any incitement to buy a Formula 1 Ferrari, that glorious moment in its brief history provided lashings of it, along with the chance to sit in the same seat as a genuine hero of mine. For anyone unfamiliar with the father of Jacques, he had a reputation for total commitment on the track, always going for broke even if the odds were against him.

When I watched this car in 1978 it looked like the ultimate racing machine. Two decades later I was taken aback to hear a mechanic at Goodwood call it "the old girl", but it has retained its quintessential Ferrari character - the crisp box and the engine sound are still extraordinary.

I hadn't realised the absence of the T3 in my life until Adrian Hamilton rang me and pointed out the omission. He had managed to prise it away from a hairdresser with a chain of salons in the north of

England (it was a case of Hair by Michael, Car by Adrian). Part of the deal, and another attraction, was that the car was booked to appear in an exhibition in Canada in memory of Villeneuve; Adrian pointed out that the guaranteed income would represent a handy discount on the price, less his commission of course.

We duly sent the Ferrari over, but following the exhibition the organisers attempted to make some savings by avoiding the air freight option, and - apparently unaware of the fate of the 'Titanic' - decided unilaterally to ship it back across the high seas. The unthinkable happened, and the freighter was holed. The only plus point was that it didn't sink, otherwise somebody would have had a nice line in diving holidays for Ferrari enthusiasts.

The crew managed to limp the ship back to Rotterdam, where problems with salvage claims and insurance took up weeks if not months. Meanwhile the poor car sat desolate in a container in the docks, its magnesium castings gently decaying. These kind of storage conditions were definitely not recommended in the owner's manual. However, for the first and only time the financial consequences of the rebuild were at somebody else's expense.

Unfortunately that blissful arrangement could not last. When the band were on tour in 1994, and I could not drive the car myself, I decided to run the T3 at the Goodwood Festival of Speed. Mike Wilds, an excellent driver who I'd entrusted with a number of cars, took on the drive, but one

The 312 was made only 15 years or so after the delicate Lotus 18, but progress was more obvious still. Gone were the welded steel tubes which made up the chassis and in their place was a riveted aluminium box designed to stay stiff and accurate in the face of grip from wide slick tyres and the pressure from aerodynamic wings. The driver was now even more a part of the car, lying ever further back and belted in so tight that movement of anything other than feet and arms was impossible. So much so that his personal space has to be engineered to fit the individual. The tiny Villeneuve had the luxury of a seat moulded specially for him. I can just fit within the square sides of the aluminium chassis, padded by bits of foam and rolled-up coat, while my right foot wedges solid in the footwell when I try to move between accelerator and brake. Nothing for it but to take off my stiff, comfortable, fireproof boot and swathe stockinged foot in yards of gaffer tape. My toes should then be free to curl.

Firing the flat 12 engine is now a familiar ritual of fuel booster pumps and slave batteries on wheels outside the car and, once started, it is the driver's job to manage the engine and keep it running. The pumps and ignition take a fair bit of power and the car's on-board generator is small and lightweight. Let the revs drop below the 3,000 rpm mark and the engine just fades to a gentle halt. Once running, the boost pump can be switched off and the engine-driven one can take over to feed a weaker mixture. The flat 12 will stop spitting and coughing.

Getting in and belting up, replacing the top bodywork and warming the engine all takes time. No longer is it possible to vault the cockpit side, flick a magneto switch and signal your helpers to push start. The driver is now technician and systems manager as well as wheelman. Driving from rutted paddock to smooth circuit, I notice, too, how firm the suspension is, enough that my foot bounces helplessly on the effortlessly smooth throttle pedal. I notice how nervous the steering feels even at paddock pace. The front tyres, which are level with my helmeted head, are at least double the width of anything I have been able to see so far and yet the wheel is unnervingly effortless. Once on the circuit, the car's response is unpredictable; first it will push as if the road is suddenly wet, then it will grip and the nose will dart towards the apex. Meanwhile, the 12 cylinder engine feels gargly and rough. It has started to spit again as I try and accelerate gently, coughing and juddering as I bring the revs up through 4,000, then 5,000. This point, though, is where the engine changes its tune.

Until then, the engine's sound is unmistakably 12 cylinder Ferrari, despite the hawking and spitting. A hoarse braying with an underlying crackle - you get the click and rush from the 12 inlet trumpets from within the cockpit, while from behind you get the wail of the exhaust, but at 5,000 it's as if a switch has been thrown. All the noises swell in unison and the wail becomes a crescendo, exactly as the car's gentle wafting forward

Ferrari 312T3

small mistake turned into a major accident, injuring Mike and damaging the car. There was consternation in the camp as to who should break the news to me in America. In fact I'd already been alerted by my daughter Chloe and so, when the phone call was finally placed, I could derive some small pleasure from listening to the lengthy pre-amble that paved the way for the bad news.

After assessing the damage it was clear we would need some help from the Ferrari factory in Italy as some components were so badly damaged it was impossible to replicate them. Thankfully I had by now established a relationship with the factory and after lengthy discussions about locating and borrowing original drawings, Ferrari felt the best solution would be for them to take over the project. The car was shipped out to Maranello where they carried out an immaculate rebuild; on this, its first subsequent outing, only the wind-screen was yet to be delivered.

When they sent the car back, the result was stunning. It was a fantastic gesture that I certainly wasn't expecting and it seems poor recompense that I can only reciprocate by guaranteeing the Ferrari factory free tickets and T-shirts for life.

turns to a giant shove in the back. At this early stage in the driver management process, the metamorphosis is frightening. The rear tyres which you see rolling round like two oil drums in your mirrors are stone cold. This matters less on the older sports cars with their extra weight and longer wheelbase, or the newer ones with their huge area of down-force, but as the ultimate of its age the 312 weighs just half a ton with an engine that pushes out over 500 bhp. When it is running hard, it generates more force than a sports car twice its size. It relies more on its tyres than anything I had tried so far.

The 5,000 rpm watershed kicks the tail wide as swiftly as a racket hitting a tennis ball and the nervous steering feels all too eager to handle the reverse lock which is an instinctive reaction. The Ferrari wobbles, darts nervously back the opposite way and makes its driver feel like a passenger, ill-equipped to drive it fast. Worse still, the gearshift lives up to expectation. Ferrari drivers have allegedly been fired for expressing opinions about this, but I sympathise. Flicking the lever forward and back is a delight, the faster you do it, the more seamless the change. Anything across the gate though is a matter of chance. Surely it can't have been like that when Villenuve drove it.

Stick with it all. Rack up some laps before quitting. And gradually the steering settles down. I begin to trust it and use the wheel to aim the car rather than steer it. I have to, because the corner is starting to happen much more quickly, and from my prone position, I can only see a small part of it. Aim the car past instead of at the apex and by the time I get there, it will feel right. The kick of the tail has now turned into a yaw. A sensation of movement rather than a wild slither. Release enough of that glorious wailing power that lurks between 5,000 and 12,000 rpm and you can still make it stray, but now it seems natural, a part of the cornering process rather than something to be feared and avoided.

I begin to look forward to each corner with eager anticipation. Unlike the sports cars which have to be persuaded and cajoled to carry their greater mass through the corner, I can just rely on the Ferrari's front end grip to point the nose. It's a delicious sensation, each time ignoring my senses which say it can't be done, each time going into the corner that little bit faster and then delighting when the car does the work. Now, the sideways forces through Club Corner begin to tug at my head while the thrust of that glorious engine adds to the total pulling against the neck muscles. I think of the heroic Villeneuve at somewhere like Monaco, several notches up the scale, but relying on that same sensation of trust to commit himself to the tunnel at three figure speeds.

I realised too, that the Ferrari was still an ultimate tool, despite its age. By the end of the 1970s, tyre and aerodynamic technology had advanced such that you could no longer balance the car solely according to the messages coming back to your hands and body. You had to trust its capability, rely as much on this as the car does on its warm tyres. No longer was the Formula 1 car something to be played with and explored at leisure by gentlemen in shirts and ties. It had already become a formidable racing machine.

Ferrari's T3 design was a development of the T series started in 1975, and featured a brand-new chassis, with suspension tailor-made for Michelin's new radial tyres. The power of the engine was also raised and its centre of gravity lowered.

The T3 was revealed at the 1978 South African Grand Prix, and at the US Grand Prix Gilles Villeneuve, driving this car - chassis number 034 (picture below) - led until he clipped Clay Regazzoni's Shadow and spun off. After performing well all season, Villeneuve won the final Grand Prix of the year, the first ever held at Montreal's Ile Notre-Dame circuit. Jean-Pierre Jarier in a superior-handling Lotus 79 was forced to retire and Villeneuve surged through to grab an historic hometown victory. He finished ninth in the Drivers' Championship that year. More recently the car has been driven in demonstrations by Jacky Ickx, Jody Scheckter and Carlos Reutemann.

Ferrari 312T3

Specification	
Engine capacity/configuration	2992 cc/12 cylinders horizontally opposed
Valve gear	Double overhead camshafts per bank
Power	510 bhp @ 12,400 rpm
Power to weight ratio	870 bhp per ton
Transmission	Rear drive, 5 speed and reverse, non-synchro transverse transaxle
Tyre sizes	Front: 920/220 x 13/Rear: 150/260 x 13
Wheelbase	2560 mm (8 ft 5 ins)
Track	Front: 1620 mm (5 ft 4 ins)/Rear: 1559 mm (5 ft 1 in)
Brakes	Hydraulic disc
Length	4274 mm (14 ft 0 in)
Width	2128 mm (7 ft 0 in)
Height	1016 mm (3 ft 4 in)
Weight	596 kg (1312 lbs)
Front suspension	Independent, rocker arms, inboard coil spring/damper units
Rear suspension	Independent, radius arms, parallel links, coil spring/damper units
Top speed	190 mph approx.
0-60 mph	3.0 seconds

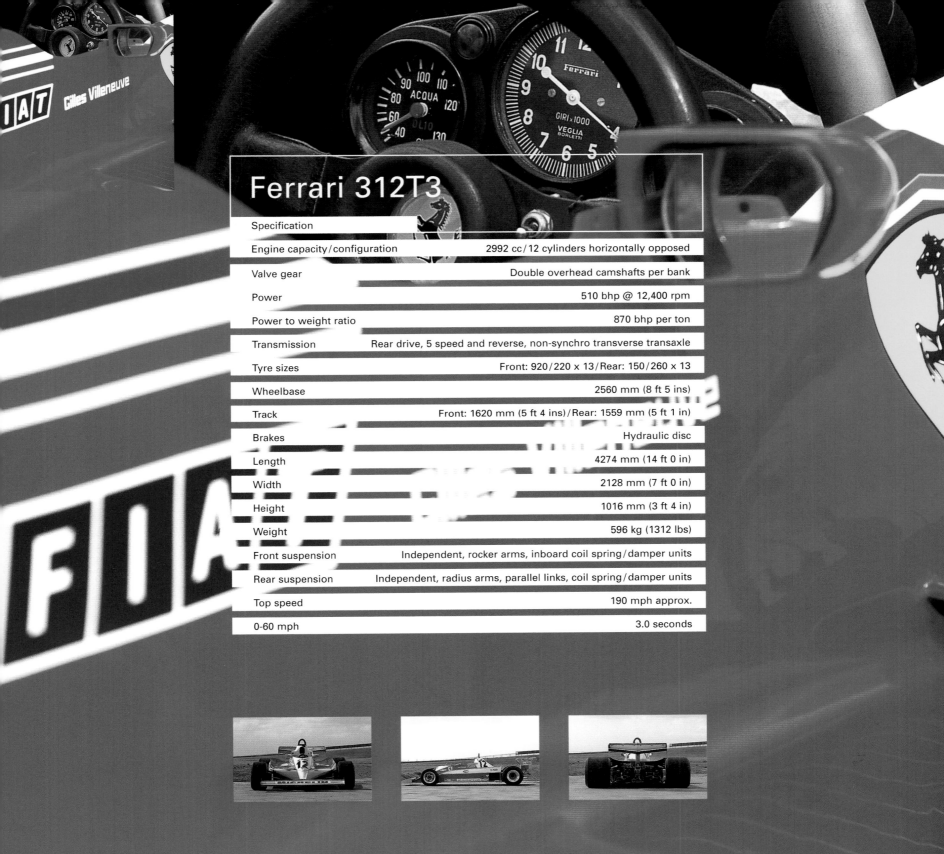

Ferrari 512 BBLM   1979

Overnight accommodation

B

y the time I got to the 512 BBLM, I had already marvelled at the GTO's perfect balance and seductive steering feel, and I had appreciated the progress that was represented by the Daytona, if not with quite the same degree of affection.

I had also driven the purpose-built 512S, which I knew might have spoiled me. From the outside, the BBLM already looked so much bigger and less agile with its overhanging nose and great long tail, two extremes which made the central accommodating part look even smaller by comparison. But when the time came to drive, the cockpit turned out to be just as comfortable and equally light and airy despite the closed roof. This would not be the last pleasant surprise that the BBLM had in store.

Starting is road-car easy and the 5.3 litre engine crackles into life at the turn of a key, but because the 12 cylinders are laid flat, the mechanical noise, thankfully, is feet away rather than inches. And yet as the engine burst into life I began to feel the first sense of 24-hour purpose in the car. Gone was the silken howl of the Daytona, and neither was there the hoarse yet musical braying of the flat 12 in the 312 Formula 1 car. Instead there's a harsh crackle from the four open exhaust pipes - a sound oddly unlike any of the other 12 cylinder Ferraris.

Out on the circuit, the 512 certainly feels heavier than all the rest. The steering takes work and feels not so much weighty but more as if it won't be hurried. You turn it and the response from the car's nose is leisurely. The whole car leans as it corners - not a great lurch like some soggy saloon, but a measured and gentle response to cornering forces. As I build up the speed, though, this sense of working at its own pace seems to extend to the whole chassis. The cornering process begins not at the nose, but from a place behind my seat. The whole car feels now as if it is sweeping its nose round a radius slightly wide of the cornering line. You sit somewhere in the middle and enjoy a sort of majestic, armchair command of proceedings.

This comfort extends to the ride as well. The 512 BB floats over bumps in similarly grand style and deals with kerbs and ruts in the paddock with complete disdain. After a few more laps, I begin to see that this is not so much an easy option in the spring department, but more a clever suspension balance; the car doesn't feel so much soft as well integrated. As if all the forces acting on it have been ranged against each other until they cancel themselves out and leave just enough of a hint of what's going on to keep the driver informed. Taut is the word.

In 1979 I left England in the spring to drive down to the south of France and start the recording of 'The Wall'. Our manager Steve O'Rourke came along for the ride. Since I had been entered to race in the Lola T297 at Le Mans that year, we stopped off en route to have a look at the circuit and to see what I was letting myself in for.

I stared with alarm at the Mulsanne straight stretching away into the distance, but succeeded in masking my fear sufficiently for Steve to think he was missing out on a good thing. Within a week he had managed to organise himself a drive in this particular Ferrari, entered by Ecurie Francorchamps, and in the race unsportingly finished higher up the field. Having enjoyed the experience so much Steve then bought the car from the team and decided to run it himself in 1980, using Bob Houghton and Rosso Racing to prepare the car.

Power, which is available in abundance from the 12 cylinder engine, won't disturb the car's flow either, maybe a slight sway from the tail and a little rise in revs if you hoof it much too early in the corner, but once again the car won't be hurried. In fact the only thing that will upset its composure is trying to brake too late. The bumps on the entry to Stowe Corner at the end of Silverstone's Hangar straight will then send some kicks back through the Ferrari's wheel rim - which is thicker than those of the Daytona, GTO or 512S - and if you ignore those messages and press harder still, the 512 will finally lock a wheel in protest. Gradually, though, the 512 makes you change your driving style to suit. Soon you begin to aim at a point way round the corner, getting ready to sweep the car all the way through the turn rather than mount an attack in current-day aggressive, slick-shod style.

Adding to this majesty of progress is the panorama flooding in through a screen which, as with the 512S, sits so low that the dash beneath is almost at knee height. And like that mid-engined ultimate, the Porsche 962, the Ferrari doesn't feel as if it is moving forward, rather that the road ahead appears to come pouring into the cockpit. The horizon tilts right or left depending on which way you turn.

Wheel and tyre problems produced a series of terrifying blow-outs at maximum speed on the Mulsanne, culminating in a particularly massive one that took out most of the rear bodywork - and probably the driver's nerves.

To keep the car going Steve's team borrowed the entire rear body section of the Bellancauto 512 which had crashed in the first hours. They completed the race in a fetching livery of Ferrari red, green and gaffer tape.

It all took a fair bit of effort, mind you. The steering definitely required arm muscles rather than a flick of the wrists and the brakes needed a firm push despite a constant need to look after them. The gears and their gate were typically Ferrari and although there was no ghastly sequential lock they would bruise the palm long before they ever shed any teeth. It was all part of the car's leisurely demeanour. And if all this lack of drama suggests that the 512 BB was a slow old thing, the lap times tell a different story. It was a whole two seconds quicker round the lap than the explosive, turbocharged F40. This revelation made you realise that the protest from the brakes at the end of Silverstone's straight had more to do with the speed the car had reached than any real frictional shortcoming.

The Ferrari 512 BB may have been a development of a road car, intended for sale to amateurs who wanted to tackle the great race, but it is nevertheless a factory-built Ferrari racer. That a few laps filled you with a real desire to drive for 24 hours, as well as the notion that your portion of a day and a night behind the wheel was something you could actually accomplish, shows how well the Italian engineers understood the event.

By the next year the car was virtually obsolete because of rule changes and I bought a half share in it, later buying out Steve as he looked for a more competitive Le Mans entry.

The car may look like a bit of a monster but it is relatively docile, bordering on the underpowered, and the driver is almost unconscious of its size when sitting in the cockpit. After the car's two Le Mans it continued to race for another year in a variety of paint schemes, but eventually I decided to revert to its original British racing green, an anachronistic gesture towards a bygone era of national racing colours.

The 365 BB, unveiled in 1971, was Ferrari's first large mid-engined road car, and the first to derive its name from the flat-12 'boxer' engine. It was introduced partly to counteract the arrival of the Lamborghini Countach: Enzo Ferrari attached enormous importance to the prestige of producing the ultimate road car, and felt he had no option but to reply to Lamborghini's challenge. The 512 was the derivation of these cars.

At the time Ferrari were concentrating on Formula 1, and so Ferrari's special 'Customer Service' unit supplied race-prepared versions of the road cars to independent teams. Some twelve such 512 BBs were prepared, including this car, chassis number 27577.

Supplied to a Belgian team, this Boxer competed at Le Mans in 1979 (driven by Beurlys, Faure, O'Rourke and De Dryver) finishing 12th overall. The following year (driven by O'Rourke, Down and Phillips, as pictured) it placed 22nd overall.

Ferrari 512 BBLM

Specification	
Engine capacity/configuration	4390 cc/12 cylinders horizontally opposed
Valve gear	Double overhead camshafts per bank
Power	400 bhp @ 7200 rpm
Power to weight ratio	364 bhp per ton
Transmission	Rear drive, 5 speed and reverse, synchromesh transaxle
Tyre sizes	Front 100/250 x 15/Rear: 110/270 x 15
Wheelbase	2500 mm (8 ft 2 ins)
Track	Front: 1500 mm (4 ft 11 ins)/Rear: 1519 mm (5 ft 0 ins)
Brakes	Hydraulic disc
Length	4500 mm (14 ft 9 ins)
Width	1800 mm (5 ft 11 ins)
Height	1194 mm (3 ft 11 ins)
Weight	1120 kg (2464 lbs)
Front suspension	Independent, double wishbones, coil spring/damper units
Rear suspension	independent, double wishbones, coil spring/damper units
Top speed	188 mph approx.
0-60 mph	5.0 secs

Lola T297   1979

Exploring the envelope

Lola T297

So many people had said the little Lola would be good to drive that the wait for a feeble November sun to dry the track was more frustrating than usual. That said, it was as well we had the time.

The apparently inevitable comedy performance trying to coax life from a small Ford engine unfamiliar with Arctic temperatures occupied most of the morning. Come coffee time, an industrial space heater had already been blasting hot air at the Lola's nether regions for a good half an hour but this alone was not enough. Time after time, the mechanics would squeeze petrol from a washing-up liquid bottle, directing it down the four trumpets sticking from the engine's head like a quartet of hungry cuckoo beaks while a wheezy starter borrowed from some long-dead Ford Cortina grated a few reluctant revolutions. Time after time the engine would cough, splutter and spit before lapsing back to sullen silence.

Sometimes the spray of petrol would catch light, galvanising the attendant acolytes, one huffing and puffing at the flames, another threatening with a large fire extinguisher. The ritual was repeated endlessly. Another thirty minutes passes and non-believers might have been tempted to abandon proceedings and head for a warm workshop. The converts meanwhile persist with the zeal of those who have done this many times before. Gradually, the engine's coughing spasms grow longer but unlike some unfortunate consumptive, more hacking and wheezing means that the Ford is not dying but slowly warming to its intended task. Then, suddenly and without any intermediate stage, it bursts into raucous life. Crisp and instantly responsive, it's as if all the previous preamble has never happened. Within seconds, the engine settles to a contented hum while the needles on the gauges start a weary climb round their respective scales.

The Lola's tapering wedge of a body only stretches as far as shin height so it's another laid-back ride in store and it's odd how lying ever longer in a succession of cockpits begins to change your perception about what is to follow. You are definitely strapped to the Lola rather than in it but there's much more in the way of riveted aluminium and firm fibreglass all round me. I know I am about to travel faster than before, but somehow I feel less vulnerable. Bend the head forward to catch a glimpse of the front wings, see the brown flakes and cracks where the tyres have rubbed and burnt through from underneath. Grasp the tiny wheel that looks hardly bigger than the instrument faces behind it, and get ready to go.

Auguste César Bertelli, the owner of Aston Martin in the 1920s, and the man responsible for the manufacture of my much-loved Ulsters, died in the autumn of 1978. I had taken LM21 to the funeral as a farewell, and got talking to Brian Joscelyne, an Aston Martin enthusiast and competitor. Brian asked me if I'd be interested in going to Le Mans as a driver. I was taken aback. Although that had long been my aim, I felt it was a goal for three or four years in the future. With an inbuilt tendency to caution, I was astonished to hear myself say yes. The offer was irresistible.

The following spring I went down to meet the team for a test day on a hill climb, which turned out to be nothing of the sort, just a seat fitting in the Lola. The next time I was going to be at the wheel was at Le Mans itself, a steepish learning curve considering most of my previous racing experience had been in one and a half litre cars from the mid-1930s or outings in the GTO. Brian said it wouldn't be difficult, "just quicker"... I did, nevertheless, take the precaution of some instruction from Simon de Lautour's school at the Paul Ricard circuit.

Lola T297

Fortunately the Lola proved to be the most wonderful little car, and the perfect introduction to Le Mans driving. I was also lucky to be with Dorset Racing who, although a small amateur team, in fact included many regular Le Mans competitors (I was driving with Birchenhough, Joscelyne and Richard Jenvey) and contained more expertise and race craft than some of the works teams. Dorset was run on a shoestring, but it was an extremely high-quality shoestring. This was proved conclusively when we finished second in class in 1979, winning the index of performance, and third in class the following year - after which I decided to acquire the car. After 4,000 miles of track testing it would have seemed churlish not to have bought it.

My first chance for practice that first year was at 6pm on the Wednesday evening; it was all quite alarming, especially with the 935s howling past. Going out in the actual race was the realisation of a number of ambitions: to compete at Le Mans and to race at night, with the incredible sensation of coming up over the rise after the pits, seeing the lights of the Ferris wheel ahead and then hitting the

The starting pantomime only needs to be performed once and thereafter the Ford engine barks into life at the touch of the starter. The four cylinder drumming that I felt from the Lotus 18 tickles my tightly belted shoulders, but not as harshly. Reach for the gearlever. Three inches of aluminium beside my knee feels loose and vague and all sorts of apparently unrelated clonkings come from behind as I waggle it. The gears could be anywhere. Search for first. Lay the lever almost horizontal till it rests against the thigh, and pull back. Feel the grating as the teeth engage. Hope that's number one...

It is. The clutch catches me out with its sharpness and minimal pedal movement, but the Ford copes, burbling down to 1,000 rpm on the flickering chronometric tachometer. Squeeze the throttle pedal. It moves a long way compared with the clutch, feels silky smooth. The Lola surges away. Tap the clutch and push the gearlever away to the right and forward for second. The stubby lever already feels much more accurate now we're rolling. The engine winds up, past 2,000, then 4,000 rpm. Still smooth and still pulling. The bark from behind begins to take on a harder edge as we pass 6,000. Another second and 7,000 rpm passes beneath the needle. Now I feel a sudden extra surge, a bigger force pressing against the shoulders. Past 8,000 rpm. The bark has turned in to a chainsawing howl. There's barely a tingle of vibration now. On to 9,000... then another 500. Like an auctioneer pressing the punters to financial excess. I know the Ford will go to ten, but I don't do it. Everything is singing. The gargling chord from the intake trumpets just behind my shoulder has reached a hoarse tenor. Surely the cylinder block of this power unit didn't start life in a Cortina... did it...? Reach for third gear.

It can be mine as quickly as I like. Don't think about it, just do it. It's a deft flick of the wrist - the more relaxed the arm, the faster you can move the lever back. Tense the muscles and it slows the process. Don't try and find the slot, just aim the lever, there's no effort. Straight back from second to third. Forward at 45 degrees from third to fourth. Then straight back again for fifth.

Lola T297

Familiarity begins to relax my grip on the lever and I find myself throwing the tiny gearknob like a dart from an open palm. I pull it back with fingers curled rather than clasped to speed the flick. The lever is still floppy but that doesn't matter. Don't think about it. Just aim in the general direction and it will find your gear for you. Each time it does, that wonderful crisp engine will be straight back to work, sweeping you along. Gearshifting seems so quick and so natural now that you wonder how you ever doubted it.

The straight is running out. Squeeze the brake pedal. It's firm but pliant. It moves just enough to let you feel how much brake you need, but doesn't grab. Smell the fibreglass burning as the body sinks on to the tyre tops. Down from fifth to fourth, then to third. Faster than it takes to read the words. Ease the wheel right. Already I have savoured the darty feel of the Lola's flat wide nose. The feeling that the whole car sidesteps rather than steers in response to the slightest squeeze of the wheelrim. And yet it's not nervous. Now it's time to take advantage, make it all work for me. Feel the left corner dip as I aim the wheel, squeeze back on the power and snick back up through the gears. I know I can go faster next time...

And I do. I brake less and later and lean harder on that front left tyre. Still no drama. Faster still then... carrying yet more speed into the corner. The difference between the straight and the turn is getting less every time. Maybe I won't have to go down that extra gear. Surely the Lola must have a limit. But how will it arrive? Will this be the moment that the car finally shows its teeth? Faster and faster. I begin to feel the only drawback of a prone driving position. Bending the head forward against the forces of slipstream and cornering is harder work than you expect, and as the body tenses against the same forces, the diaphragm squashes the lungs and makes you breathe shallow and quick. Time to visit the pits for a few moments' reflection.

The Lola is the fastest car of all so far. It has modern slick racing tyres and an aerodynamic body with a rear wing to press the car to the track. It has the best part of 300 horsepower from the two litre Ford engine... I must remember to use the left footrest in the corners. As soon as the foot clears the clutch, I must slide it left and push on the rest. Brace the body, free the muscles in the chest and stomach. Let the lungs fill more easily, make a better support for a head made heavier by a full-face helmet. Be more a part of the car rather than a tensed-up addition to the seat.

brakes hard before driving past the fairground through a heady bouquet of brake pads and frying onions. Achieving a good finish was more than I had dared to expect.

It also provided one of my biggest racing frights when, trying to check on the faster traffic coming up behind me, and with the mirror blurring, I turned my head to glance behind me on the Mulsanne straight. I'd been warned not even to raise an arm into the 170 mph slipstream but had forgotten this advice. The airstream caught the edge of my helmet and wrenched my head back agonisingly. It was a salutary lesson.

In 1980, when my co-drivers were Pete Clark and Martin Birrane, the weather was worse, and the race much harder work. On my first driving stint I spun the car, and later, around midnight, a different drama occurred when a hose carrying the clutch fluid ruptured. After some minutes trying and failing to improvise a mechanical solution, I climbed back in and managed to run the car on the starter off the grass and onto the track. This could now be construed as a dangerous position, obliging the marshals to push the car to safety. This was all I needed to restart the car and get back to the pits.

The whole Le Mans experience was exhilarating - I loved it. When the race was over, I rang my mum to let her know I was still alive. She said "You will be careful when you drive home, won't you?"

Time for one more session, and to research the outer limits once and for all. I now know that the big numbers on the tachometer - nearly twice the amount of revs available to the Aston or the Alfa - is the band where the engine works best and the seemingly endless activity of gearshifting is the necessary means to keep it there. The trip up and down through the box is now a process of thought rather than a conscious action. I know, too, that the brakes and the slick tyres need to be hot in order to work and, as with the Ferrari 312, each lap is quicker as the tyres get stickier. Meanwhile, it takes a little extra time to trust the car's chassis balance and its ability to carry speed into the corner. Every time I exit Stowe Corner, a little voice still whispers "You could go faster there..."

And, sure enough, every lap is faster than the one before. Not because the limit I have been waiting for is infinite - like any car the Lola does indeed wag its tail or push its nose when you demand too much from tyres and suspension - but because the balance between front and rear is so fine that you can steal a little from one end to help the other. Better still, you can experiment in relative safety because the car won't bite.

Braking ever later for Stowe finally makes the tail stray as I turn. So I try braking just a little earlier and more gently. Give the car an instant to settle, then take the speed with me into the corner. The excess brings the first hint of protest from the nose. Not a scrabbling inelegant lunge for the outside kerb, but a gentle easing wide of the intended line. Next lap, I try keeping the speed but bringing on the power earlier, just as I start to ease the wheel. Normally, this would be a recipe either for a big tail slide or a big push from the hard-working front end, but neither happens. Instead, the balance returns and with it, the temptation to carry yet more speed and accelerate even earlier. The real key is the car's willingness to let you lean ever harder on that front tyre, because you notice that, unlike the older cars, the car is not drifting at an angle while all this is happening, it is simply going faster through the bend.

Reluctantly I climb from the Lola, my head a ferment of how and where, my senses still tingling from the sheer pleasure of slipping, sliding and steering, and the challenge of how much of each to try. The bark of the engine is still fresh in my mind. The changes in pitch and density as the revs climb and the way the flow of noise dips seamlessly with each gearshift before climbing immediately back to where it was before are inseparable from each variation in cornering technique. In some ways the facility to unsettle and balance with a combination of steering and throttle felt much like the Lotus 18, but the difference is that the Lotus demanded large amounts of such treatment in order to perform at all and punished you if you got it wrong. The Lola has so much more grip from its slick tyres but invited you to try your hand, then rewarded you if you got it right. Inviting - that's the word.

Lola T297

Specification	
Engine capacity / configuration	1950 cc / 4 cylinders in line
Valve gear	Double overhead camshafts
Power	290 bhp @ 9500 rpm
Power to weight ratio	511 bhp per ton
Transmission	Rear drive, 5 speed and reverse, non-synchro transaxle
Tyre sizes	Front: 820/220 x 13 / Rear: 140/230 x 13
Wheelbase	2330 mm (7 ft 8 ins)
Track	1340 mm (4 ft 5 ins) front and rear
Brakes	Hydraulic disc
Length	3860 mm (12 ft 8 ins)
Width	1800 mm (5 ft 11 ins)
Height	792 mm (2 ft 7 ins)
Weight	576 kg (1267 lbs)
Front suspension	Independent, double wishbones, coil spring/dampers
Rear suspension	Independent, lwr wishbone, top link, radius arms, coil spring/dampers
Top speed	190 mph+
0-60 mph	4.7 seconds

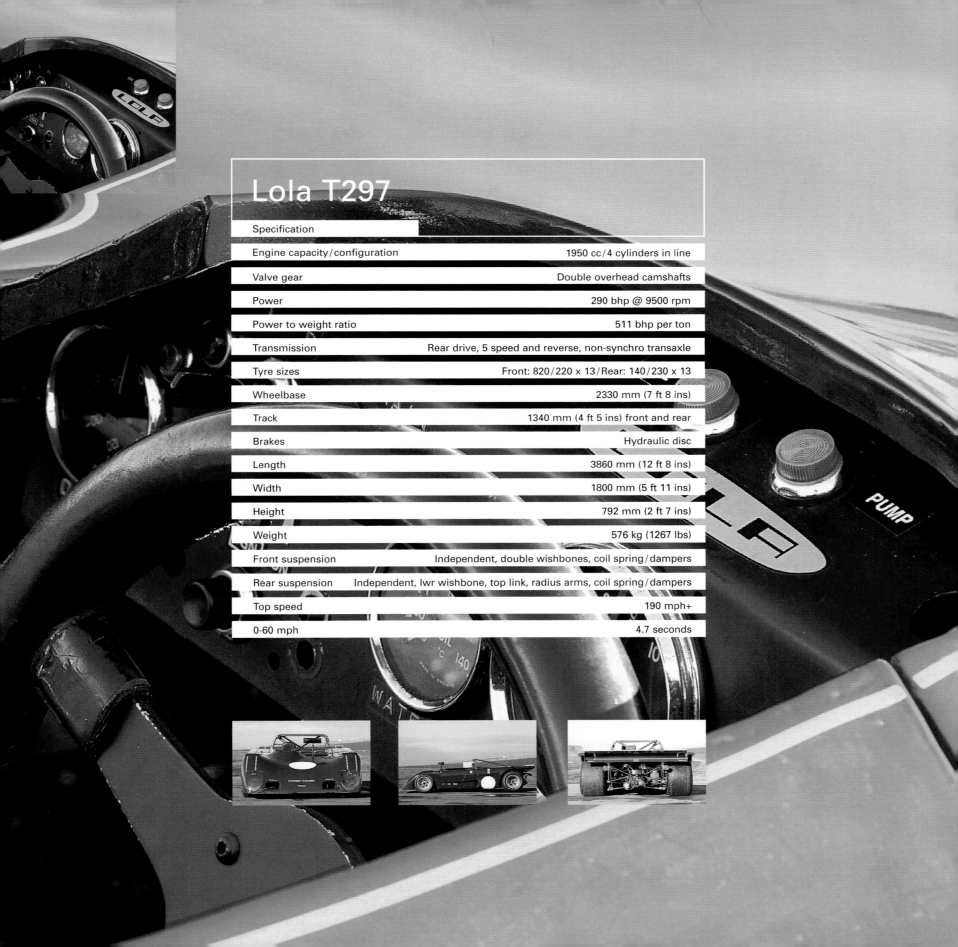

Tyrrell 011   1983

The professional age

My experience with the Ferrari 312 was a reminder of how relatively complicated Formula 1 cars had become. Nothing like as much as they are today, but compared with the ERA or Maserati 250F there was a vast amount to adjust.

As well as the infinite variety of springs, roll bars, shock absorbers and overall geometry, there was the novelty of aerodynamics, which, although at a relatively early stage in its application to cars, was an infinite variable. Just a few laps in the Maserati made you understand that going fast was up to you. Nothing whatsoever was adjustable, so you alone had to work out how to use it best.

By comparison, even half a day spent with Nick's Tyrrell gave me no chance to feel completely comfortable, or to extract more than a percentage of its potential. Many have been the Formula 1 teams who went extremely well during winter testing, then stumbled at the first race because they didn't get all the settings right throughout a Grand Prix weekend. The Tyrrell also served to underline what the Ferrari had already suggested. In addition to the army of engineers required to adjust and maintain these cars, the speeds and the consequent forces on the driver's body were now so much greater than they were in the early years. It was no longer possible to race these cars effectively as a true amateur.

But even if Formula 1 was already becoming an exclusive arena, it was still possible to build a car to compete using proprietary parts from English engineering companies. Anyone with the money could go and buy a DFV Formula 1 engine from Cosworth Engineering in Northampton, England. That same well-heeled individual could also go to Hewland Engineering in Berkshire and buy the gears to transmit the engine's power. Ken Tyrrell, one of Formula 1's great survivors, had done just this, then conceived a simple aluminium honeycomb tub to accommodate his purchases before using his team's experience to ensure the range of adjustments was right on the day.

This approach shows in the 011's construction. The car has a neat air of simplicity and it looks so much smaller than the Ferrari thanks to a more compact V8 engine, an in-line gearbox and smaller sidepods. The chassis tub is deeper and narrower too, which makes it harder to get in. No room for a seat, of course, which also makes me think that driver size was becoming another exclusive criterion. Especially as the bulkhead which supports the front suspension has an opening big enough to pass legs through, but not both feet at the same time.

Once in, the driver lies back even further and is now more than ever part of the car, which is intimidating at first. The bodywork is taller and tighter round the shoulders and arm movement yet more restricted - only my forearms and wrists are free to move. I can see nothing at all behind except whatever the tiny mirrors can reveal and yet the front wheels seem close enough to touch.

My first drive in the Tyrrell was unforgettable. During a general test session at Donington the traffic slowed noticeably; I thought it must have been stopped because of an incident and I'd missed the red flag. In fact, the Tyrrell was so quick in every form of movement that the rest of the cars seemed to be moving in slow motion.

My affection for Tyrrells probably started when I watched Jackie Stewart winning World Championships in various earlier versions. I first bought a couple of the 1978 007 models after they had been raced in the Aurora series (for recently superseded F1 cars), but when I acquired the 1978 T3 it seemed mildly excessive to have three cars from the same season.

Then I was offered the 1983 011. Unusually, no dealer was involved and the car was ready to run - it came direct from the factory via John Dabbs, who had worked with Tyrrell as an F1 team engineer and was now working with me as a full-time mechanic. John knew the car and still maintained a working relationship with a number of the technicians on the team.

In addition, the 011 was one of the last DFV-engined cars: the change to turbo power had ruled the normally-aspirated DFVs out of Grand Prix competition for ever. This fitted in with my theory that it is usually better to have the last, and generally definitive, version of one type of car - when all the problems have been ironed out - rather than the prototype of a new car. Turbo technology increases costs considerably and demands the addition of a laboratory full of bespectacled boffins. And the other mandatory requirement - a bull-like neck able to withstand the G-forces generated by more power and more down-force - would have required a complete wardrobe of shirts with larger collars.

This is one car I still haven't managed to race... Racing a Formula 1 car demands as much commitment as I made to sports car racing in the 1980s and I don't have the inclination to go back. It's not just a question of finance, with the constant engine rebuilds and the changes in tyre compounds, it's also to do with the huge amount of time you have to spend on set-ting-up, testing and adjustments. Amateur testing is even worse: it takes three times as long as the professionals do to work out what changes to make. I belong to an older school who prefer to saunter up, pull on some string-backed gloves and set off with a jaunty wave.

Starting the Cosworth V8 follows the Ferrari's procedure. Pump and ignition on, then a raised hand and twirled finger tell the mechanic to key the starter. The V8 feels much harsher at low speeds than the Ferrari did, sending high-frequency vibrations through the whole car. You feel the tingle through the wheel's rim, and the buzzing from the rear bulkhead sets me coughing again. There's none of the Ferrari's spitting and snuffling, though. The V8 revs up instantly whether cold or warm. Gearlever is in the same place, but there's no gate, and this at first seems like an omission. The lever flops about through at least 90 degrees and you can't sense which one your fishing hand has caught. Remember the Lola technique - don't think about it - aim the lever rather than try and select a slot.

The day is freezing, and now there's more to add to the sense of intimidation. It's as if the track has turned to ice, because those big slick tyres offer no grip whatsoever. I try and build a little speed to get some temperature, but the nose darts and jinks in response to the slightest movement of the wheel, then judders and pushes wide of the apex. The slightest squeeze of the throttle pedal drives the car forward for a few yards then, as the engine climbs up the scale, the power suddenly breaks the rear end loose. You get one chance to catch it. Let the revs build too much or allow the tail to stray more than a few degrees and the car swops ends more quickly than you can imagine. Not like a slide which gets away from you, giving your brain time to keep track of what's happening, but like being hit from behind by a truck. Sudden, vicious and inexplicable.

Modern Grand Prix cars never race in freezing cold conditions, but if there's a cold test session, the moment the car comes to rest, mechanics immediately wrap electric blankets round the tyres. Without them, it's a case of gently, oh so gently, building the speed, trying to lean on the front tyre and take more speed with you, then accelerate just that tiny bit earlier in the corner.

The transformation from snapping, twitching, bad-tempered beast to precision racing tool seems to take forever but is actually about five or six laps. You begin to feel the car settle and you promise yourself that you really will leave the braking that bit later next time, will definitely take the next turn that bit faster. Now the Tyrrell's rear end is suddenly calm. Feels glued to the track and treading the pedal ever earlier in the corner unsticks the front instead and makes it push wide. Is this because the 480 horsepower coursing through the fat rear tyres has warmed them more than the narrower fronts? Or is it time for an adjustment? Difficult to tell. I realise, though, that braking too late always makes the front push, and if you persist, the inside front wheel stops turning. Suddenly, out of the corner of your eye, you can see the maker's name on the tyrewall and see the bits of debris that a sticky slick has picked from the track. It's an oddly contrasting image, because every-thing else in your vision is vibrating with motion. Mustn't let the mind fix on it. Off the brake to loosen the wheel, then back on and hope you make the apex.

The chassis is not as immediately friendly as the Ferrari's. It feels more as if the ends of the car are reaching their working state at different times. Maybe I need a degree or two more wing, a few millimetres more nose-down rake, some softer springs, some stiffer bump settings on the shocks. Maybe it's just the temperature. More than ever I realise that this is a complex machine and I'm not going to experience its full capability.

Despite that, the car feels as if it's beginning to work with me. The tingling from the V8 engine moves forward in the car as the rasp from the Cosworth turns to a strident scream and the tiny tacho ahead sweeps towards 11,000 rpm. I don't cough any more, but now my legs are buzzing. It may not be as classy as 12 cylinders and the noise is harsh rather than musical, but there's no doubt that the engine pulls from almost tickover to beyond 11,000 rpm without so much as a spit or a snuffle nor a surge or step in the flow. The gears, too, turn out to be so very easy to use. Up, down, across the gate and back is as fast as you can make it and you can miss out as many gears as you like on the way.

Grand Prix cars were about to enter the turbo era when the Tyrrell was made. Soon it would not be possible even to start the engine without the manufacturer's representative and his computerised briefcase. Special fuels would be needed and aerodynamics would become the dominant science. The Tyrrell was one of the very last of a dying breed. A car built from proprietary parts and capable of being run on an occasional basis. I wish I'd had more time with it.

The 011s appeared halfway through the 1981 Grand Prix season - that they appeared at all was remarkable given Ken Tyrrell's problems with a shortage of sponsors, and the constant adjustments which designer Maurice Philippe had to incorporate to keep up with the regulations imposed that season.

In 1982, after yet more rule changes, Philippe's team reviewed virtually every component, lengthening the chassis, and introducing new rear suspension, consisting of rocker arms at the top and a wishbone below.

This car, although purporting to be chassis 05, maybe 06, since it has the machine-turned bulkhead peculiar to this car as well as various other unique features. Both 05 and 06 were driven by Michele Alboreto, 05 finishing third at Imola and 06 delivering a marvellous victory at the final meeting of the 1982 season in Las Vegas (picture above) and giving Tyrrell his first Grand Prix win since Patrick Depailler had triumphed at Monaco in 1978.

Tyrrell 011

Specification

Engine capacity / configuration	3000 cc / 8 cylinders in vee
Valve gear	Double overhead camshafts
Power	500 bhp @ 11500 rpm
Power to weight ratio	942 bhp per ton
Transmission	Rear drive, 5 speed and reverse, non-synchro transaxle
Tyre sizes	Front: 105/230 x 13 / Rear: 150/260 x 13
Wheelbase	2720 mm (8 ft 11 ins)
Track	Front: 1740 mm (5 ft 9 ins) / Rear: 1600 mm (5 ft 3 ins)
Brakes	Hydraulic disc
Length	4190 mm (13 ft 9 ins)
Width	Front: 1770 mm (5 ft 10 ins) / Rear: 1645 mm (5 ft 5 ins)
Height	950 mm (3 ft 1 in)
Weight	540 kg (1188 lbs)
Front suspension	Independent, double wishbones, pull rods, coil spring/dampers
Rear suspension	Independent, parallel links, top rocker arm, coil spring/dampers
Top speed	185-190 mph
0-60 mph	2.9 seconds

Ferrari F40   1989

On thin ice

Much has been written about the Ferrari F40 and much of it by me. Before we got together again for this book, F40 NPG and I had already spent a fair few hours in each others' company.

Together we were once holders of a joint world record, listed for all to see in The Guinness Book of Records and although a hundredth or so less than four seconds to 60 mph sounded impressive in 1990, it didn't tell the whole story. Much more exciting than the frantic sprint to 60 was the subsequent progress to 170 mph and beyond, followed by the wrestle to get the Ferrari stopped before the test track ran out. The print-out from the electronic measuring equipment said we had taken 22 and a bit seconds to reach three miles a minute. Now, for a road car, that is what you call fast.

By comparison, the record-setting run had been almost disappointing. The F40 had struggled off the line, turbos fast asleep, the V8 engine temporarily unboosted. A second or so later, the whole lot had exploded like some hitherto smoking volcano. The rear wheels had spun crazily while I worried about the impending and awkward dog-leg movement required to select second gear. As a drag race, the whole thing had been pretty indifferent, but before I could attempt another, one of the turbos developed a boost problem. Already, though, the car's character had been clearly defined. Like a caged tiger, the F40 is cuddly and benign when dozing but can wake in an instant to become a whirling ball of terrifyingly savage energy. There seemed to be little in between.

I was forcibly reminded of this while lapping a cold, damp Silverstone early one morning. Driving gently round while the various oils came up to temperature, the Ferrari seemed innocent enough. The passage over the bumps felt taut and controlled rather than merely stiff, as if the body moved in harmony with the wheels rather than twitching in response to ripples in the road. This feeling of self control was reminiscent of the GTO, but more insistent, as if some invisible force was constantly pressing and adjusting from outside. As it did so, messages unhampered by the numbing feel of power assistance begin to feed back through the elegantly simple black-rimmed wheel.

A touch lighter in the turn says that a puddle has robbed some grip from beneath the tyres, a kickback there tells you that a painted kerb has come and gone. The F40's steering is not as telepathically informative as the 1962 model's and it needs more effort thanks to huge modern tyres, but it still talks a tongue exclusive to Ferrari. I remember thinking that last time I tried it the F40 possessed some of the best steering feel available anywhere. That was before I tried the GTO.

This was the first brand-new Ferrari I bought. I had been determined to ensure my name was high on the list for the F40, even considering a name change to Aaron Aardvark in case the decision was based on alphabetical order. It was probably no drawback that David Gilmour also wanted one, and that we were playing in Modena soon after the car was introduced in 1988. We managed a visit to the test track at Fiorano, enjoying an afternoon being driven in the prototype: it was hard to decide whether the car or the hot-shoe Ferrari test driver was more impressive.

Although the cars were initially intended to have various optional extras, by the time the F40 was in production there were about as many as Henry Ford offered on the Model T - not even a choice of interior finish. The only decision was whether to take the customised luggage or not. The Schedoni company make all Ferrari's leather luggage, and their range for the F40 was beautiful, but minimal - a slim suit carrier, a miniature briefcase to wedge under the passenger's knees and a round hand-tooled suitcase just the right size for a deep-crust pizza.

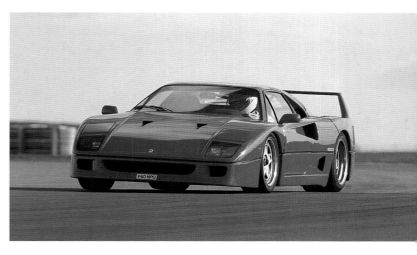

Meanwhile, from behind, there's not the rumble and rattle of a traditional American V8. Instead there's a lazy hum like a slow revving four cylinder whose drone mixes easily with the thump and boom that reverberates around the simple, thinly trimmed cabin. The seats within are deep race buckets, thinly padded to push back and hold against the firm clamp of wide, full harness belts. Dials are few and borrowed from something small and humble nestling in the FIAT corporate parts bin, along with the switchgear. None of this matters, however, any more than the pull cord to open the doors. Together with the starkly functional carbon fibre weave of the door sills, it somehow says this is a car without compromise.

By now, the gauges are alive and the fluids warm enough to work. So I tread the throttle in third gear through the exit of Club Corner. The hum grows hoarser, and then turns without warning to a bellow. The rush is unbelievable - the F40 starts to hit you in the back, then thinks better of it. The rear wheels lose their grip of the cold greasy track and the rev counter flicks round to the rev limiter. It happens quicker than it takes to read. Frantically I release grip of the steering to let the car's castor wind on reverse lock more quickly than I could fumble at the wheel, but the tail is quicker still. Dip the clutch and hope. The F40 gyrates through 180 degrees almost within its own length, then gets ready to charge the barrier backwards. Fortunately, my brain has now caught up with events and I remember to brake. This has nearly happened before, but somehow I don't remember it being quite so inevitable from so early on. Before, it had always seemed possible to get a slide going and, with judicious use of the throttle, to keep it there.

I tried again. Tried to keep progress smooth above all else. Again, there was that lazy hum followed by an explosion of wheel-spinning energy, even when you weren't trying. Maybe it was the November weather freezing the grip from the tyres. Maybe the puddles were deeper and the tyres' tread less so than when I last sat in that deep and grippy seat, but whatever I did, boost equalled wheelspin, which equalled more revs which equalled more boost which made it impossible to drive neatly. And it would all happen in any of the first four gears. There was just not enough grip to deal with the difference between natural and boosted states.

Time for a pause to allow time for the track to dry a little and to reflect on the sheer chameleon energy of the F40. It wasn't that the steering was too slow - nor, hopefully, the driver - but simply that once rear tyres a foot wide had both broken grip then the rear end was on castors. Meanwhile,

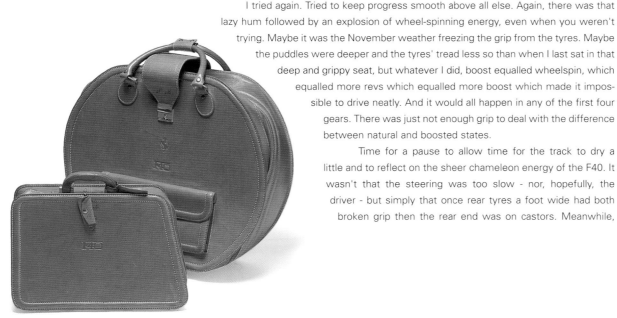

Dave and I went back to pick up our cars later in the year. The only problem was that Ferrari insisted on giving us lunch at the Cavallino opposite the factory gates, and it was late afternoon before we could get away. Dusk - and snow - was falling as we were trapped on some awful mountain pass in the Alps, with juggernauts threatening to lose control and crush the pristine carbon-fibre nose. Going downhill was worse, as by now it was pitch black. My co-driver was Bob Houghton, and that was the moment we discovered that there was no interior light or torch, so we were unable to find the de-mist switch or read the map.

The only casualty of the trip home was Bob's licence, which he had to surrender for speeding to the French traffic police, who were clearly deeply patriotic and Renault supporters rather than Ferrari enthusiasts.

Ferrari F40

I got enthused enough about the F40 to start reinventing elements of it, including a re-designed rear screen to see the blue flashing lights behind more clearly. I believe this car has one of the highest mileages of any F40 but like to think this makes the cost per mile much cheaper than all those cars which have been mothballed since new.

The moment I remember most clearly in this car was when we left the Ferrari factory, headed out of Modena and reached the autostrada. Once we'd cleared the tollgate I just pushed the throttle and was pressed back in the seat as the engine wound up and we took off like an F16 plane from an aircraft carrier. As with the GTO, one of the pleasures of the F40 is sitting beside a guest expert like John Watson or Peter Gethin and enjoying their surprise when they experience this power in a road car. The sensation is just as thrilling, even after all these years, and the car still gives me enormous pleasure when I get out and look at it. It makes nipping out for a pint of milk a lot more fun.

as I waited, some of the F40's other features came to mind. Almost as much as the engine's explosive energy, the gearshift dominates cockpit proceedings - more so than any other Ferrari I have tried. The long chrome-plated lever with its simple round black knob sticks up from the slotted aluminium gate and while at rest it seems to click in and out of the ratios easily enough. Once on the move, though, the synchromesh seems to change the feel of the whole action. You hear the lever clicking and scraping at the metal gate, but the action has grown sticky, like trying to cut fresh Parmesan with a blunt knife. You press, the cheese gives and then if you are lucky, the blade slips through. The feel is unique to Ferrari but, far from being a minus point, it adds enormously to the satisfaction of driving the thing. Moving the lever accurately so that it doesn't hit the edge of the gate and hang up the change, moving it fast enough that the revs don't fall away and then have to rise again when you let the clutch up, moving it slowly enough that the synchro doesn't try and spit the lever back out again, all of these have to be at an optimum. Make no mistake, a smooth Ferrari shift is a rewarding thing in itself.

But, back to the track, now dried and warmed a little by a weak winter sun. A few corners and an exploratory prod of the accelerator showed the volcanic energy was still ever ready to erupt, but now it had a channel. The tyres had recovered some grip and although they still struggled a little in first and second, the sheer exhilaration as you sent the first and sharpest spike of torque through third gear and towards the exit of Club Corner was a rush that is hard to beat. A slip as the tyres gave in to the onslaught, a kick of the tail to the left calling for a touch of reverse lock, then a kick in the back as the rear tyres grip again. Straighten the wheel, feel the tail sit down and the nose rise up. Your head meanwhile goes back and forward, left to right, bobbing against the force. Nearly 8,000 on the tacho calls for a shift to fourth almost before the corner is fully unwound. Head helplessly forward as the force dies away, turbo wastegates whistling and wheezing as they vent the surplus boost. The force returns with the next gear, seemingly

The F40 was the last new car produced by Ferrari and personally overseen by Enzo Ferrari before his death in 1988. Originally intended to be a limited edition of 750 cars, it proved so popular that Ferrari produced nearly double that to satisfy demand.

This car, chassis number 078122, was - along with the car bought by David Gilmour - one of the first privately-owned F40s in the UK, and has one of the highest mileages. In 1990 the car took part in the Pomeroy Trophy at Silverstone (picture above), the competition devised on elaborate formulae to try and establish the best all-round touring car, by testing performance, manoeuvrability - and luggage space. Sadly, the standard rectangular wooden box used to test the latter wouldn't fit the space designed for the F40's customised cases, dropping it down the running.

This particular F40 did, however, hold the record for 0-100-0mph, set at Santa Pod in November 1991, with a time of 15.9 seconds.

undiminished by the taller ratio and your head goes back yet again. The whole car becomes a surging, writhing, rocking ball of energy and assaults every sense from balance to hearing. Please, can we tread it just a little too early at the next corner, just a little mind you, so we can feel it all again. But not enough that we might spin. Go on, you know how much. You can do it...

The Ferrari's wonderful turbo V8 dominates the car, and it is difficult sometimes to believe that it displaces just 2.8 litres. But this perhaps is its only shortcoming. The delicious surge as the turbos turn the engine from low-compression idler to explosive racer is more than even big tyres and clever suspension can always cope with. Merely 500 rpm extra on the rev counter wreaks a change from nice Dr Jekyll to dangerous Mr Hyde and a slightly bigger engine with a little less boost might have made the transition more gentle. Some of Nick's other cars lapped faster, and there were cars which accelerated quicker - although not by much. There were better-handling cars and there were more friendly cars. None, though, gave the same feeling of dancing on thin ice. The feeling that you could drive all day at a gentle pace if you wanted to, but that the door to dangerous addiction could be opened with a squeeze of the right foot. Any rush is potentially addictive, but the F40's is bigger than you'll get from anything else on four wheels.

Ferrari F40

Specification

Engine capacity / configuration	2936 cc / Twin turbo-chargers, 8 cylinders in vee
Valve gear	Double overhead camshafts per bank
Power	478 bhp @ 7000 rpm
Power to weight ratio	442 bhp per ton
Transmission	Rear drive, 5 speed and reverse, synchromesh transaxle
Tyre sizes	Front: 245/402R x 17 / Rear: 335/352R x 17
Wheelbase	2451 mm (8 ft 1 in)
Track	Front: 1595 mm (5 ft 3 ins) / Rear: 1610 mm (5 ft 3 ins)
Brakes	Hydraulic disc
Length	4430 mm (14 ft 6 ins)
Width	1981 mm (6 ft 6 ins)
Height	1130 mm (3 ft 9 ins)
Weight	1101 kg (2422 lbs)
Front suspension	Independent, twin wishbones, coil spring/damper units
Rear suspension	Independent, twin wishbones, coil spring/damper units
Top speed	201 mph
0-60 mph	3.9 seconds

Porsche 962　1990

Feel the force

Somewhere between Chapel Curve and Stowe, I caught the motion of a hand waving to my left. The wiry young man squatting in the 962's passenger space was unhappy about something.

He shook his head and motioned once more with his outstretched hand, then like someone fearful of losing their balance, clamped it back to the dash top. Car sick perhaps. Surely not. This was a hardened sports photographer and well used to such things.

Back in the pits, he explained. "I was really afraid that I'd fall over on top of you..." he said ruefully. "I didn't want to stop, not at all, but after only a lap, I just couldn't push hard enough to keep myself off the dash. I can't believe how much force there is when you hit the brakes..."

I already knew the 962 would be way quicker round the lap than any other of the cars capable of carrying more than one - even the fine balance of the little Lola could never match this twin turbocharged 600 horsepower pink wing with its roller slick tyres - but just how much quicker, I had yet to take in.

This was partly because the 962 is designed to go fast for long distances and to do that it must preserve the staying power of its driver. While I was soon aware of the forces tugging at my head and body, the seat seemed soft yet firm, like a favourite arm-chair, ready moulded for my dimensions. The belts were pulled tighter than should have been comfortable but the webbing was wide, so their pressure was dissipated, and there were plenty of vents and ducts to blow cool air if the day were hot. And all the controls were easy to reach; the gears in the huge gearbox way out aft were equipped with synchromesh like a road car's, and there were screen washers, demisters and heaters. The vertically opening doors shut and sealed with a nice firm clunk and the dash which had been gripped so firmly by my recent passenger was neatly finished with furry black fabric.

From outside, the cabin had promised to be tiny and claustrophobic - the seat seemed a long way towards the centre of the car - but once across that wide sill, with body ensconced deep in the seat and legs safely threaded way down under the screen, it was immediately a seductive environment. Seductive but unfamiliar. You get no sense of the car's hugely long tail and you can see nothing at all abeam your shoulders or behind you. Peering out through the steeply curved screen from way back in those all black quarters was like seeing the light at the end of a tunnel. Remote yet somehow involving, it all made you feel like the pilot of some alien spaceship, a perception heightened by the expanses of flat wide bodywork stretching way out ahead beyond and below your line of sight. That you could already be so comfortable with such performance at your command had to be some kind of testament to the technology at work.

It was my experience with the Porsche 956 that made me want a 962 - they're virtually undistinguishable, although dashboard enthusiasts would appreciate the 962's extraordinary array of displays giving you information on every aspect of the car's performance (and probably the weather conditions in Stuttgart).

My introduction to the 956 came in 1984 when a film director friend, Mike Shackleton, came up with what was undoubtedly a brilliant idea. He persuaded the Rothmans team to let us make a film based around my enthusiasm for cars and called 'Life Could Be A Dream'; as part of the deal I was to be given a drive in the team. This was living with the gods - or at least hanging out with them in a motorhome.

The first drive was in the 1000km race at Silverstone. I'd been working in Germany the night before and arrived on the day just in time for practice. Not perhaps the best preparation for such a drive, even with all the massages and high-energy drinks offered by the Rothmans team trainer. It's noticeable in some of the out-takes from the film, when I'm commentating while driving, that my voice suddenly dries up completely as I spot the tyre marks describing a beautiful reverse circle to record some other driver's monumental drama. At the Mosport 1000km in Canada, driving with Vern Schuppan, I like to think

The 962's most significant science, though, is invisible. The giant aerodynamic hand that presses the car firmly to the road and allows you to brake and corner at a speed your brain suggests is impossible. You get some early hint as to the size of the force from the stiffness of the springs that have to withstand this pressure - you see and feel the nose bob up and down over the merest crack in the road as you drive round a paddock that you had thought was unbroken tarmac. And yet when passage of air over the body begins to weigh it down, the ride is smooth. The car seems to float through the corners, gently rocking from corner to corner in a lazy rolling motion that seems completely unrelated to the car's speed and the sideways forces pushing against your body.

Back out again and alone in the cockpit, this is a car whose ability you have to trust. Massively stiff suspension designed to cope with a 100% increase in body weight when the aerodynamics start working doesn't give you much in the way of feedback. The Lola's delightful and instant response to a touch of the wheel is nowhere to be found. Instead you have to commit the 962 to some point way round the corner, looking far ahead up the road, turning earlier and aiming the nose way, way ahead. Sitting in that dark cockpit with no sense of anything but the ribbon of road ahead of you, it's almost as if you are stationary and the road is unfurling like a coiled whip slowly shaken free.

I begin to sense that the Porsche carries nothing like the same percentage of energy as the Lola going into the corner, but has the ability to harness double the power from its twin turbo engine on the way out. The speed at which the Lola enters the turn is almost frightening and the cornering force is no more than you expect. The Porsche feels more leisurely at first, but gathers speed at a breathtaking rate as you negotiate the bend. The early turn you soon discover is necessary, because the 962's front doesn't bite at the bend, it begins to devour it. That early commitment, aiming almost out of sight beyond the apex, is vital because the twin turbochargers take a moment to spool up and feed the engine. If the nose were to bite early on, the engine's eventual outpouring would kick the tail somewhere between Finmere and Oxford.

Tread the unbelievably powerful, tireless brakes, feel the belts tighten as your chest pushes against them. Gently snick the gearlever against the synchro and let the box drop down a gear. Start the turn well before you feel is right, aiming the spatulate snout right round the corner. Tread the throttle. Hear the turbos whistle, feel the ever-increasing surge. Feel the force that will try to straighten the wheel, building up. Relax the shoulders, let the lock unwind gradually, see the kerb on the exit sweeping towards you. Suddenly you realise how much speed you have gained since you entered the corner. The acceleration tugs your head bac,k while the cornering force that has so quickly built up tugs it sideways. Straighten the wheel. Feel the rear end shuffle as the transmission sorts the power between the huge rear slick tyres. Swiftly but smoothly push the lever away for the next gear...

Later that day, I watched Barrie Williams running past the cameras, and it struck me how long the car looked, how the cockpit was so close to the front wheels, and how much the tail hung out behind the rears. The car seemed to turn from a point just aft of the front wings and it was as if the rest of it was some kind of baggage that had to be trailed behind. I could also see the nose nodding and bobbing before the corner, something I had only really felt over the bumps in the paddock. Also odd from outside was the sound of the engine. The Porsche's

we might have made the Top Three but we were asked to relinquish our battery to the leading Rothmans car. It was clear that in a team including Bell, Ickx, Belloff and Mass, N. Mason was not high up the priority list.

Three years later, preparing for a race at the Nürburgring, I was able to extract a BMW from Avis, and had the immense bonus of some private tuition from Derek Bell. You couldn't ask for a better teacher to guide you round the 13 miles and 72 corners, many blind. We duly returned the car to Avis with an enormous mileage and every fault light illuminated.

At the 1984 Le Mans, Rothmans withdrew the team cars, unhappy with the regulations that year, but instead gave support to Richard Lloyd's Canon team. My co-drivers were Richard himself and René Metge, who had won the Paris-Dakar, one of the toughest of all rallies, the year before.

When the production run of 962s was coming to an end, I thought it would be a good idea to buy one and hand it over to Richard to run at Le Mans. It was nearly as alarming being an owner as a driver, torn between issuing instructions to drive as fast as possible in the hope of a place or to take it easy and preserve the car. It seemed appropriate to keep the car in exactly the same configuration as it finished Le Mans, complete with scrutineering stickers and sponsors' decals. This car has a number of unique features. No dealers involved, no restoration or modification, and with less than 3,000 miles on the clock and just one careful owner maybe the guarantee is still valid....

cylinders lie flat across the car, three to a side, with one turbo per flank, each with its own exhaust outlet. You only hear half the engine's voice and despite the motor's willingness to rev to an indicated 8,000 rpm and more, it only sounds like half that amount. A droning baritone with a splattering lisp at the edges like a vintage tape recorder's hiss, it doesn't stir the senses like some of the older engines... You can also hear each turbo at work through the very short exhaust pipe. It whistles as the turbines spin up, chatters and chivvies like a monster sparrow as the valve in the wastegate opens and closes. The 962 sounds more like some high-tech earth mover than a Le Mans winner.

Driving the Porsche is much more of a management exercise than most of the others. The Lola you take for a dance, you lead and it follows in some kind of intimate partnership. The Porsche you lie back and operate, much like a modern fighter pilot. You have to, because the technology that ensures both power and mechanical stamina is too complex a combination to respond in an instant. Nevertheless this technology has been made nicely driver-friendly. The gears are smooth and easy to operate - not as quick as those in the Lola's Hewland, but somehow in keeping with the lazy power of a turbo engine. The clutch too is light, as are the brakes which you have taken for granted but which have never wilted or grumbled and yet proved strong enough to defeat the arms of a fit youngster inside a lap.

The Porsche is awesome. As much for its ease of operation as its enormous performance. A 935 with all its quirks fixed. Turbos, chassis, wings, the whole lot working together in perfect harmony. The more impressive because it can repeat the performance, lap after lap, for a day and a night without so much as a hiccup.

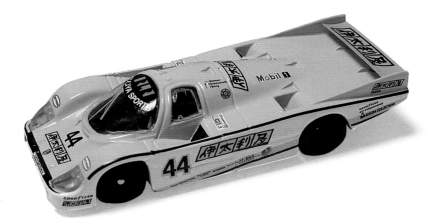

Porsche dominated Le Mans throughout the 1980s with the 956 and its successor the 962. There was little difference between the two models, other than the driving position, set slightly further back in the 962 in a bid to improve driver safety. The cars were extraordinary, not just because of their record of success, but also because relatively large quantities of private customers could buy and race the cars - a Porsche support team providing the necessary back-up.

This car, chassis number 962/161, was bought new from Porsche in 1990, and delivered to Richard Lloyd just in time for its debut at that year's Le Mans - the pink livery was part of a sponsorship deal with Italiya, a Japanese sports clothing manufacturer. Driven by John Watson, Allan Berg and Bruno Giacomelli, it finished 11th overall, despite problems with the brakes and overheating. This was the car's first and last competitive outing.

Porsche 962

Specification	
Engine capacity / configuration	3164 cc / Twin turbo, 6 opposed cylinders
Valve gear	Twin overhead camshafts per bank
Power	670 bhp @ 8300 rpm
Power to weight ratio	755 bhp per ton
Transmission	Rear drive, 5 speed and reverse, synchromesh transaxle
Tyre sizes	Front 300/630R x 17 / Rear: 325/680R x 17
Wheelbase	2771 mm (9 ft 1 in)
Track	Front: 1605 mm (5 ft 3 ins) / Rear: 1600 mm (5 ft 3 ins)
Brakes	Hydraulic disc
Length	4800 mm (15 ft 9 ins)
Width	1998 mm (6 ft 7 ins)
Height	995 mm (3 ft 3 ins)
Weight	902 kg (1984 lbs)
Front suspension	Independent, twin wishbones, coil spring/dampers
Rear suspension	Independent, top rocker arms, coil spring/dampers, bottom links
Top speed	240 mph
0-60 mph	3.6 seconds

McLaren F1 GTR   1995

One step beyond

K40 MCL

It was annoyingly familiar. Six years had passed since our last car test, and here we were, back at Silverstone, and it was raining again. It wasn't just drizzle, but successive deluges, each of them biblical in its intensity.

Nick's McLaren F1 was ready and waiting too, but I was dragging my heels, checking a leaden sky for a promise of blue. Memories of the F40, whose wheelspin soared uncontrollably whenever the turbos were awake and whose back end skittered equally uncontrollably in response, were forever etched on the memory... But then maybe the McLaren would be different. There were no turbos to spiral up and skew the engine's power delivery just when you didn't need it, and besides, you already knew Gordon Murray was a genius, so perhaps he had found a way to adjust the laws of physics. The F1 was, after all, built as the ultimate, usable supercar, so it could just be. Track time was ticking away, so there was no choice but to find out.

Nick's car is part racer, part road car and the roll cage is a perfect ape-hanger on which you support the body weight while you swing your legs all the way to the middle of the cabin and over the seat's edge, point the toes beneath the steering wheel, then flop into the bucket. It's then you see the sense of a central driving position. The pedals are dead ahead, there's no wheel arch to shift them one way or another and the steering wheel is perfectly placed to hold with gently bent arms. It helps as well that the carbon fibre tub is just that. A large space defined by right-angled slabs of composite, there's nothing to interfere with the legs or feet, not even any carpet. To your right is the stubby lever for the six-speed McLaren-built transmission, ahead is a small screen which is the need-to-know dash and your only source of information.

The starter whirrs urgently in response to the twist of a key and the engine springs immediately to life, but somehow it doesn't sound like a V12. Rather than the organ chord of legend there's a harsh, bass-heavy growl which sends a hum through the structure, overlaid with a strange moaning which rises and falls in harmony. Who knows whether it is cams, gears, the rush of air disappearing down inlets or the fusion of scalding energy exiting from the twelve exhausts, or a concert of all. Like all the multi-cylinder engines in this book, the BMW engine has its own completely distinct, many-layered sound beneath which you hear the less happy rattle and screech of the racer's option; straight-cut gear teeth, clattering like a spin drier filled with bolts.

I first met Gordon Murray in the 1980s through Chris Craft, when we were frightening ourselves at Le Mans with the Dome DFL car. I was impressed. Here was a Formula 1 World Championship-winning car designer who was also mad about music. Equally impressive was the fact that, at the time when everyone else in F1 was clad in corporate uniforms, Gordon continued to sport a pair of plastic sandals in the pit lane.

Some time later I heard that he was designing a road car for McLaren. According to Gordon I said to him, "If you're going to do a good new supercar, you'd better try a good old supercar first." As an outsider I was very flattered when he took me up on the offer, knowing the rigid veil of secrecy that surrounded the whole project. Given Gordon's huge knowledge of auto technology it was a joy to get his feedback on cars like the GTO, F40 and Zagato Aston.

I enjoyed feeling that I might be of some use to his project, and at his request jotted down some notes on the cars. In particular Gordon had explained to me he had a pathological hatred of car radios, and so I introduced him to the idea of the (relatively) new CD jukebox.

Gordon remembers: "Nick was bloody useful. I have very strong, polarised views on sports cars: the instruments are usually illegible, the feel of the gear change no good, the pedal layout useless. My team was young and relatively inexperienced. They hadn't owned many sports cars. Nick was able to give me some direct, practical input. For example, on the Ferrari F40, he said that what is annoying is knocking the spoiler off every time you drive into the garage, because the car is so low to the ground. Against all my better instincts, I made the F1 higher off the ground. And since the cars aren't used daily, Nick suggested a remote battery charger that could trickle-feed in the garage - something I've since copied on all my cars."

Although I was intensely interested in the gestation of the F1 road car, I didn't put my name down for one of the production models. A million dollars was a frighteningly extravagant amount of money for a new car - ten times more than I'd ever spent before, and I'd also just thrown away the deposit on a Jaguar XJ220 that suddenly seemed a less than good idea, so I was feeling more than usually cautious.

This extraordinary cacophony hunts and grumbles its electronically prescribed sequence while everything warms, and should you try and go before it has, the screen will wag a digital finger and flash its disapproval. Five minutes or so later and the ridges en route to the track rattle and clonk the suspension's joints, then it's out to splash through the puddles where the first thing you feel is the massive and instant response to the accelerator. There's never anything like a big engine in a light car to give a sense of complete omnipotence, but when travelling gently this one spins up and dies away so very quickly that smooth gearchanging is very difficult indeed.

The pedals move effortlessly beneath the feet but, inevitably, I seem to flare the revs before the clutch is home or whizz the engine far too high when trying to match the speed for a downchange. Add to that a gearshift which is slightly sticky across its three-plane gate and I feel like I've forgotten how to drive. Meanwhile my fears for the wet are fully realised. The F1's steering feels oddly light and lifeless despite the absence of power assist and I fidget with the rim, searching for some message which will let me know whether the front tyres have grip or not. More research via a gentle, exploratory tickle of the right pedal sends the nose washing away from the corner. The slightest extra pressure lights up the rear tyres and kicks the back end wide just as if we'd hit a patch of ice.

I'm desperately trying to get some rhythm into this. If only I could lean a bit more on that front end, then I could carry some speed without using so much power. The tyres wouldn't spin and the two of us wouldn't skate. Not that I'm using more than a fraction of the grand total. Slip, slide, hear the growl turn to a harsh rattle as the revs soar, and when they reach 7,500 rpm, the peculiar harmonic which you hear as well as feel, thrumming through the carbon structure and into the seat... Persist for a few laps in the hope I might find a way and then, at last, the front begins to show a little more interest. Maybe the rain is less than it was, maybe the tyres have squeegeed some water from the track and are cutting through to the tarmac. Perhaps they are getting a little warmer. Road tyres aren't supposed to need heat, but there's no doubt the front end is working better and that seems to be the key to progress.

Even then, you need care because it still only takes a fraction too much right foot to spin up the rear wheels and time after time I feel the clonk as the steering reaches the opposing lock stop. That's when you find the wheel is not a living thing like the F40's and you can't let the castor spin the reverse lock for you. It has to be piled on by hand. There's another trap emerging too. This dose of confidence tempts you towards the corner and makes it all too easy to lock up the front wheels under braking. By the time you have them rolling again, you'll pitch into the corner a few miles per hour too fast and the tail will come slewing round.

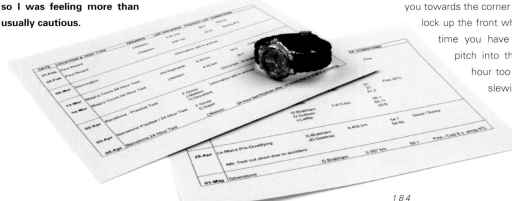

I did have a chance to drive an F1 briefly, though, and it was stunning. My first impression was of its size. It lacked the lumbering dimensions of most supercars which required docking rather than parking, and of course its performance was sensational, with a truly rocket ship-style sense of acceleration.

However, in the mid-90s, with the development of the GTR as the racing version of the F1, my interest was rekindled. I love the link between road and track. And from a practical point of view, race-designed cars tend to be much simpler to look after for an owner, with fewer of the complex electronics that require a degree in computers to fix when they go wrong.

I also realised that I owned a car I really didn't need, a McLaren M15 which I had spent years trying to restore. It was also a car that Ron Dennis did not yet have in his McLaren collection. So for two or three years, Ron and I feinted and parried, with Gordon as a benign intermediary, while Ron intimated that he didn't really need the M15, and I gave the impression I could manage perfectly well without an F1.

Eventually I broke, and the car I now have, chassis 10R, appealed the most of three lurking in Woking. I liked the fact that despite its lack of actual racing history, there was complete, detailed document-ation of the testing noting all the aces - including in particular J.J. Lehto - who had driven it. The link to Le Mans was absolute.

It hardly seems like the perf-ormance of an ultimate - and it's difficult to work out the exact reason. The handling of the car isn't freakishly difficult; at this reduced speed it is usually possible to hang on to it. And unlike the F40 which metamorphosed into a savage froth of energy in its own time, the McLaren at least gave you notice. You knew when a wayward moment was coming, but there simply seemed to be insufficient grip to allow access to the car's reserves. I began to wonder if the halfway house between race and road car is not achievable, and that on a wet surface the suspension settings might be way too stiff for treaded road tyres. Photos done, there was nothing for it but to return on a dry day.

When that came, there was better opportunity to appreciate the purity of Gordon Murray's creation and realise that it is beautifully made. Your gaze cannot help but roam over all the sculptured brackets and mountings. They have been hacked and turned to gold by technology rather than the skill and sinew used for the Bugatti or the Alfa 8C, but equally impressive in their own way. Survey the beautifully fashioned bunches of bananas which carry the exhaust gases from the massive 6.1 litre V12 BMW engine, first to the catalysts, then into the silencers, which look as if they have been made as a piece of art in a similar style to the rest. Just like the Bugatti's cylinder block. You marvel at the way the McLaren's door flies upward, then slows as the gas strut reaches the end of its travel, gently clunking everything to a halt. Try it time and time again just to see if it always does. Wonder too at the perfect shut lines revealed each time you snick the door closed. It's the little touches you notice, the ones you didn't expect. Then you remember that the McLaren was fully type-approved, just like a Ford Mondeo and unlike most of its exclusive comtemporaries. You pause, knowing the effort that this must have entailed. Knowing that McLaren made just over one hundred of these. Obsessive indeed...

And so to a dry track where I'm hoping the grip that was missing will be restored and the McLaren's strengths will be usable. Immediately there's no doubting the relentless surge in response to the right foot. Not suddenly explosive like a turbocar, but unrelenting. An outpouring of acceleration that seems to have no end. You shift up, and the force pinning you to the seat seems hardly to diminish. I learn that the best way to a clean gearshift is to move the lever quickly without being brutal, more like a Formula car's dog box. You still need to be careful going across the gate, but the faster you do it, the better it gets. The steering, meanwhile, has changed its mood. There's plenty of tugging and shuffling at your fingers, but you still don't get much sense of its authority and I'm still searching for the confidence which says the car will definitely turn when I ask it to. It's better in the slower corners, but then a prod of the accelerator still picks up the nose and pushes it wide. A bigger prod still fires the rear tyres and slings the tail with an alacrity which is startling. It's the same story as it was on a wet road, but it happens at higher speed.

McLaren F1 GTR

In the end Ron treated me mercifully, and we agreed a deal in which 10R would come to me ready to drive away on the road. This involved an assortment of adjustments, including the addition of reversing lights, catalytic converters and silencers - and a horn, not normally a requirement of modern motor racing.

I picked up the car in December 1999. My daughter Holly and I went down together to the McLaren facility in Woking to pick it up, and then took it back around the M25 to North London. After juddering out of the workshop it felt perfectly tractable on the road. Later we made a few extra modifications. The rear-view vision was still a little lacking, so we added a cockpit screen and mini cameras to aid parking, and to get the depth of blue on the flashing lights struggling to keep up...

Gordon has an interesting take on this particular car. He considers the Ferrari GTO to be the last of the great competition cars that could be driven to the circuit. With the McLaren F1 having become a racing car, this prototype chassis, converted back to road use, is in his words "the modern 250GTO. It's Nick's kind of car."

I try a run through Stowe, the long corner at the bottom of the straight. Rushing towards it in sixth, bellowing, growling, thrumming, gears shrieking. Feel the grumble of brakes turning energy into heat, down two gears, careful across the gate, then forward one more to third. Try and time the release of the brakes with the first aim at the wheel, hope the gentle sway from the rear will help the nose point towards the apex so I can begin squeezing on the power. Nearly... Not too much now. I've accepted that a pair of road tyres simply cannot deal with this kind of urge in its entirety. Squeeze it on. Feel the back just rocking a touch, hear the revs rise as the tyres unstick, then grip again. See the road ahead beginning to straighten, so squeeze the pedal some more. Let the tail wag if it wants, because you're nearly done. Flatten it now, and see the dash is cycling numbers quicker than you can read them, but you get the idea that 8,000 and the limit is fast approaching. It's time to snick back for fourth before the red light blinks on the dash. Later I see that there are two black lines on the road.

Nick's McLaren is a bit of an oddity. It is lovely to look at, small enough to be usable in the real world, and its pedigree is impeccable, as is the quality of its construction. The engine is fantastic, an apparently bottomless well of power which is amazingly devoid of temperament. And there is the sense that everything has been considered and nothing has been left to chance. But you also get the feeling that as a road car, this has touched the edges of the envelope. That it would always struggle to contain and manage its own capability. The conversion to race car gave it the grip of race tyres which it so desperately needed, and the freedom to pin the nose close to the ground and keep the air from flowing underneath and lifting the car. Changing it back has left it somewhere in between. If you grabbed it by the scruff, lit up the tyres in the lower gears and drove it like a hooligan, it kind of caved in and submitted. It was just that I never really felt like trying the same technique in the taller gears...

In 1998 TAG-McLaren bosses Ron Dennis and Mansour Ojjeh were seeking to extend their industrial base beyond Formula 1. With co-director Creighton Brown and designer Gordon Murray they decided to produce the world's finest and fastest road-going sports car. The three-seat, centre-drive McLaren F1 was launched in 1992 and the first car was delivered in 1994. It was not only the world's first moulded carbon-composite production car, it was also the fastest - at 240.1 mph.

Gordon Murray designed it as a habitable road car, but two enthusiastic early clients - Ray Bellm and Thomas Bscher - persuaded McLaren to create a racing F1 GTR variant for 1995. Lighter, more powerful and with race-legal aerodynamics, the five initial McLaren F1 GTRs shone in the 1995 'BPR' Championship season. Le Mans provided the pinnacle success. McLaren not only won the 24-Hour classic on their debut, but finished 1st, 3rd, 4th and 5th. Their winning car bore Japanese backer Motakazu Sayama's 'Ueno Clinic' colours - its drivers J.J. Lehto/Yannick Delmas/Masanori Sekiya.

Chassis 10R was the 1996 lightweight GTR prototype, tested in December 1995 with uprated 6.1 litre BMW V12 engine, improved transmission and greater downforce. But it remained essentially an uprated road car design, and Porsche's new GT1 - purebred for racing only - proved superior, though McLaren's 4-5-6 finish at Le Mans 1996 remained admirable.

McLaren F1 GTR

Specification

Engine capacity / configuration	6064 cc / 12 cylinders in vee
Valve gear	Twin overhead camshafts per bank
Power	600 bhp @ 7000 rpm
Power to weight ratio	594 bhp per ton
Transmission	Transverse, 6 speed and reverse, straight-cut gears
Tyre sizes	Front: 275/35 ZR18 / Rear: 345/35 ZR18
Wheelbase	2718 mm (8 ft 11 ins)
Track	Front: 1558 mm (5 ft 1 in) / Rear: 1488 mm (4 ft 11 ins)
Brakes	Hydraulic disc
Length	4367 mm (14 ft 4 ins)
Width	1900 mm (6 ft 3 ins)
Height	1090 mm (3 ft 7 ins)
Weight	1021 kg (2226 lbs)
Front suspension	Double wishbones, co-axial coil springs
Rear suspension	Double wishbones, co-axial coil springs
Top speed	240.1 mph
0-60 mph	3.2 seconds

Ferrari Enzo   2003

Rage in the machine

The Enzo is a whole host of contradictions: the way it looks, the combination of eagle's beak and chipmunk cheeks for its nose, the half-length cockpit like a space-age pickup truck and the huge haunches apparently made for a bigger car and tacked on as a giant afterthought. A crimson peacock's tail made of epoxy resin.

And the red paint which saturates the schnozzle-heavy shape has a kind of chromed allure which richens the hue and only adds to the controversy over the styling. It seems those who like the blend of space-age insect front and chunky kit car back, and those who don't, already inhabit equal sized camps.

And the way the Enzo goes… It hardly seems like ten years since Silverstone and a Ferrari F40 which always struggled to contain the savage energy of its turbocharged engine but was all the more exciting for it. But a decade has indeed passed, and the Enzo was Ferrari's attempt to create something just as special using the technology of the time. Six years on, that too is out of date. Meanwhile, the wide-open spaces of a former Northamptonshire airfield have given way to the picturesque sweeps of Anglesey's cliff-top racetrack and if the F40 had two thirds the power and was terrifying in its brutal intimacy, the more up to date Enzo could hardly be the same, could it?

There may be a decade and a half between their respective birthdays, but both Enzo and F40 still affect angular lines, each a composite carapace apparently carved from blocks of ice rather than a skin pulled tight over muscular sinew. For the F40, the folded paper look was simply the style of the mid-80s. The Enzo, you get the impression, is this way for a more specific purpose, the squared edges defining the channels which direct the passage of air over and through its body. The invisible aerodynamic hand which will press down and secure the car to the road beneath.

It also features an engine twice the size of the F40's and with half as many cylinders again. No turbos this time but a claimed output of 650 bhp at 7,800 rpm from a massive six-litre V12 which, together with the computer-controlled semi-automatic six-speed gearbox, fills half the Enzo's length. The cockpit space is pushed so far forwards because there's no choice.

Hook the fingers under the sunken door catch and click it open. The massive structure swings up, propelled by hissing gas struts, the weight supported on a huge, forged central crank. It's a completely logical answer to the problem of wide supercars and standard sized garages. Notice the lack of trim in the cabin, the weave of carbon fibre as style rather than omission, the rubber mats fixed to the floor. Spot the seats which look more substantial than the older car's and tilt forward to reveal a small

My dad met Enzo Ferrari in the 1950s. In fact, it was none other than the great Enzo who fixed it for my father to drive and on-board film in the Mille Miglia of 1953, orchestrating all the necessary paperwork and formalities at the last possible moment. The car was a 1953 166MM Spyder Vignale – chassis 0272M, race number 514, which designated their start time at Brescia; they finished a creditable 56th. The competitors' badge still adorns my father's vintage Bentley, which is a cherished member of our family.

Eight years old at the time, I could not appreciate how important the race was, nor how special it was that Enzo Ferrari would take the trouble to organize the drive. Perhaps 'Il Commendatore' had an uncanny premonition that this would be one of the great sales coups of all time once that eight year-old finally gained access to a royalty cheque…

hammock where you can stow your toothbrush and wallet. Search in vain for the chrome gearlever and round black knob which have been a Ferrari signature for years, then look down to see just two pedals. Brake and accelerator. Gearshifting is by two paddles – right-up or left-down – each a fingertip's distance from the garish computer-game steering wheel. If the car's mechanical layout has dictated the exterior styling, electronics have to a great extent defined the cockpit.

Sliding in is easy with the sill hoisted as part of the rotating door, then haul it all down and feel the solid clunk as it closes. The simple circular crank handle at the front turns out to be a once-traditional window winder and you see why the glass is smaller than you might like – there has to be room for the side pocket below it which in turn creates room for the left elbow. The driving position, though, is perfect. Deep seat clamps me in place, frees the arms and legs to work the controls. The wheel is straight ahead and well clear of my thighs, feet in line with legs, big footrest left of the brake, padded shin rest up to the right. There's a good view through the bowl of a screen too, and almost as important, sensibly sized wing mirrors. These are details which make you relax in surroundings which might otherwise feel intimidating. The car's designers were clearly drivers too.

Now survey the rows of buttons and strings of lights up ahead, already blinking need-to-know information from the rim of the steering wheel. They are all rather less familiar, but the only ones we might need today are those marked 'R' for reverse, 'RACE' which hands back most of the gearshifting decisions which the normal mode assumes for you, and possibly 'ASR' to turn off the traction control. Pull back on both paddles to bring up 'N' for neutral on the screen next to the red and white speedometer and rev counter, and press the starter. A 12-cylinder whirr, then a proper V12 rasp comes swiftly from behind. Noisy but not intense, it's so smooth that it might come from somewhere outside the car. Hook the right paddle for first, lift up and release the fly-off handbrake and press the right pedal. The car eases forward without any more effort than it takes to tell and I am soon trundling towards the track wondering how much louder the road roar drumming at the resin body, and the rhythmic thump and bang as the huge 35-section tyres slap the gaps in the concrete access road, can possibly be.

On track and feeling my way, it's still hard to resist the schoolboy delight of hooking the right paddle just to see whether it will produce the same result every time. And every time the engine holds its rpm while the note changes from a rasp to a metallic clatter before the electronics thump the clutch back in. Not exactly lightning fast and not as smooth as a conventional auto but impressive in the way it revises the process to suit the power you use and the speed you go. Hook the left one to go down and the system revs up the engine to match the roadspeed, which is even more

So when Ferrari initially announced the Enzo project I was committed to getting my name down on the waiting list. The theory is that when Ferrari issues these supercars in genuinely limited editions, the company tries to assign the cars, almost by invitation only, to people who are going to treasure them rather than sell them on immediately for a quick profit. This is a pretty hopeless task, curiously similar to those concert tickets for 'must see gigs' that always seem to end up on eBay.

Over the years I had worked quite hard at trying to remind Ferrari that I was an ideal and trustworthy candidate. I had a decent assembly of old red motors, a complete wardrobe of Ferrari shoes, socks, jackets, shirts, hats, even wore the watch. What more could I do?

The ploy worked, and a call came to ask if I wanted an Enzo. The initial thrill dissipated slightly when I discovered that most of the English music business were also down for early cars, and further more that yet again drummers were further down the food chain than guitarists and singers. I ended up telling Eric Clapton and Jay Kay that I had turned down an early car as I'd been told by the factory that there were some teething problems – a small distortion of the truth, but one required to retain my dignity.

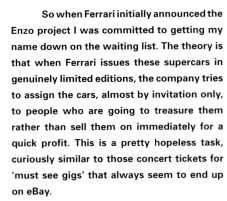

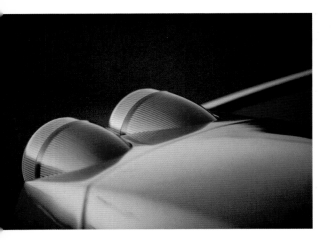

fun, especially if you are coming down from an illegal rate where the gaps between gears are wider.

All this control at your fingertips is very seductive in its modern computer-controlled kind of way, but it does take its time. Maybe it has to because the laws of physics are still immune to electronic intervention and the gaps between the ratios in a 200 mph-plus gearbox are necessarily wide. You can't zip through them like you can in a Touring Car. Within a mile, however, you realise that electronics have their benefit. Anyone could drive an Enzo, and do it with three digits and a foot. A finger and thumb to hold the power-assisted wheel, one more to hook the paddles and a foot to press the accelerator and brake. No one need ever fluff a shift or stall the engine.

An Enzo, though, is made to do much more than merely move, but in tune with a theme common throughout the lifespan of this book, the road outside is now soaking wet. It brought back memories of the F40's uncontrollable wheelspin when the turbos came in, or the sense that the road had turned to ice under all four of the McLaren F1's wheels. And any hope that the Enzo's raft of electronic technology would have an answer was soon dispelled. The brake pedal clicks and twitters while the car shuffles right, then left, the anti-lock trying to sort an expedient between ever more urgent pressure from my foot and Anglesey's Tom Pryce hairpin which is rushing towards me. Once there, the nose resolutely refuses to

On delivery the Enzo was just as exciting and exotic as it had looked in the specifications, and a huge step on from the F40. It is a fact of life that each supercar is inevitably technically outclassed by tomorrow's standard production car: the F40 is slower around a circuit than the 355 and Neanderthal in comparison to the Enzo. On the other hand, the beauty of a great supercar is a quality well beyond simple performance, and it can be rather heartwarming to know that there's a caveman lurking in the garage ready to head out and scare all those feeble new boys.

When I collected my car from West London, I received a lengthy, detailed briefing from the engineer. The Enzo has a considerable array of race-style kit: switches to flick the car into race mode and launch control, and another for implementing a jacking system to avoid losing the front splitter on traffic-calming humps (a selection of my F40 splitters maybe found at a number of roadsides around London). Unfortunately I was so overwrought at getting my hands on the steering wheel that I failed to remember a single instruction he had given me once I sat in the driving seat.

I immediately drove the Enzo out west, testing all of the buttons on offer. I think I probably had far too much fun with the launch control early on, as we had to fit a new clutch within the first 1000 miles, only to discover that this didn't come under any kind of guarantee and was considered a 'consumable'.

I have to say I am not convinced that the Enzo is the perfect road car for modern British roads. Hindered by left-hand drive visibility any approach to a roundabout would

point towards the apex, chattering and juddering across the road. I try to make amends with the one thing I know is certain and pour on the power, but the big V12 stutters, impotent in the grip of electronic interference. Despite massive modern tyres, there was not enough grip to allow even a fraction of the available power to reach the road. The electronics already knew what I could feel.

It was all too familiar. Nick's McLaren F1 had felt much the same, and I knew there was nothing to be done but wait for the road to dry. I had briefly tried turning off the traction control but the wheelspin flared so suddenly and in an instant could so easily kick the tail beyond the reserves of steering lock necessary to call it back. There was, though, the realisation that as long as I left everything switched on I hadn't had to do very much to navigate the water. I could just sit there and drive normally while the management sorted the brakes, the steering, and the power, trickling little streams of each according to the available resource most in need. The grip from the tyres.

A wait for the sun to dry the road and light up the mountains which keep a stoic watching brief from the coast opposite and try again. Tickle the right hand pedal. The car surges forward. Ease the rim and feel the nose dart towards the hairpin's apex. Wait an instant, get the car pointing nearly straight and tread the right pedal hard. There's no lag, no wait for turbos to spin up. Just a massive instant outpouring which seems to gather momentum rather than lose it. Launch towards the next corner and tread the left pedal with the left foot. Brakes were a weak point of both F40 and McLaren but the bite from the Enzo's four enormous 13.5-inch carbon-ceramic discs is massive and consummate without being sharp and jagged. The car just stops without dipping its nose or weaving, and the discs will do it time and time again.

However, what follows is a confusing mixture. The front points immediately in response to a command from the wheel, then goes limp. I try and balance with the massive power, but calling it too soon pushes the nose wider still, while opening up the turn then treading harder on the gas simply calls in the traction control which reins the power back. It's as if all the same ingredients that defined the car on a wet road are still intact but have been rearranged within an envelope only slightly larger. Turning off the traction control only makes those outer confines more uneven, the reactions more extreme and the rhythm more difficult to build. The knowledge that even Michael Schumacher's freakish talent was unable to make the Enzo lap much faster with the traction control turned off makes the point about grip with more eloquence than I can write.

The frustration that we all felt is more a sense of potential which is being denied by simple circumstance than any disappointment with the design, so we even used the test as an opportunity to try a different set of tyres. The black

benefit from a man with a red flag running ahead. It is driving on the track that gets the heart rate up. I am lucky enough to have a friend with both an Enzo and access to a current Grand Prix circuit. These are the truly memorable drives. It would be insane to give this car its head on the road, but to hit the brakes hard and shift down on the paddles into a modern circuit's corner is as close as you need to get to being a proper 21st-century racer.

Soon after my first experience at the wheel, the Enzo had an early outing on the BBC's *Top Gear*. Initially negotiations for a fee stalled, but one evening I found myself having dinner with Jeremy Clarkson. The subject of the Enzo came up, and as my Pink Floyd memoir *Inside Out* had just been published, I announced in a rather offhand way that the show could have the car for nothing if they would promote my new book. Jeremy looked pensive. Two days later he rang me back with a wizard wheeze. Since the BBC has a policy of no overt advertising, Jeremy's idea was to write something that might slide through this stumbling block as post-modern irony...

Ferrari Enzo

From the very first moment the Enzo came in shot, I was there selling my book. 'How exciting is it to own an Enzo, Nick?' asked Jeremy. 'Nearly as exciting', I replied, 'as the day my book *Inside Out* was published'. The programme continued in a similar vein.

Even better Jeremy then returned to the studio to meet ex-Spice Girl Geri Halliwell, 'So,' Jeremy asked Geri, 'what are you doing these days?' As soon as she started to mention her new record, Jeremy interrupted with, 'I'm sorry, we can't plug product on this programme.' At this the camera tracked back to reveal the entire audience wearing T-shirts saying, 'Nick is a great author' or 'Nick's book would make a great Christmas present.'. Tapes of the show are, I understand, now required viewing for trainee BBC producers, to generate discussion on the morality (or lack thereof) of such content.

wheels you see in the pictures were a set of Pirelli's road legal racers which are very much a modern fashion on high performance hardware, but while the front end had definitely gained some welcome extra bite, the rears still could not cope with the engine's massive urge.

At the same time, there was no denying the excitement that surrounds every outing in this car. The sense of occasion that floods the cockpit every time you touch the starter button. The sense of expectation that this time, I could somehow access even a part of the maximum half ton of downforce and make the tyres grip and the systems relax. Because every so often, little portions of the car's massive potential do manage to sneak beyond the restraint which keeps it safe. Like the relentless, missile-like acceleration when the car is pointing straight, and the giant ceramic discs which rob the energy of speed even faster than the engine can add it. The gearshift which handles it all for you, and the steering which adds life to the front end, albeit in a perversely remote fashion.

On the public road where the car is destined to live and work for most of its life, the regulation built in to the Enzo will still leave you with a surplus big enough to risk imprisonment or worse. It's only the freedom of a track which tempts you to unleash the car and deploy its capabilities in different areas.

There was a time when cars could handle both road and track and there are several in this book, like the D-type Jaguar, the Ferrari GTO, and even perhaps the F40. The Enzo's layout has less in common with these and more with the Porsche 962 Le Mans car of 1990, but without the grip of slick racing tyres or the downward pressure that comes from a ground clearance the depth of a matchbox, the Porsche too would have been neutered.

Complex technology needs its partners, but as long as the car needs to be road legal, legislation and cost impose different constraints. If the Enzo's potential is too finely filtered to suit the road, a set of slick tyres straight off the shelves at Dunlop, or Pirelli, or Michelin would so easily channel its resources for the track. Taking the Enzo to Anglesey was not so much a disappointment, more another lesson learnt in this extraordinary 100-year journey.

Ferrari Enzo

Specification	
Engine capacity / configuration	5998 cc / 12 cylinders in vee
Valve gear	Twin overhead camshafts per bank, 4 valves per cylinder
Power	650 bhp @ 7800 rpm
Power to weight ratio	476 bhp per ton
Transmission	6 speed, semi automatic
Tyre sizes	Front: 245/35ZR19/Rear: 345/35ZR19
Wheelbase	2650 mm (8 ft 8 ins)
Track	Front: 1660 mm (5 ft 5 ins)/Rear: 1650 mm (5 ft 5 ins)
Brakes	Hydraulic vented disc
Length	4702 mm (15 ft 5 ins)
Width	2035 mm (6 ft 8 ins)
Height	1147 mm (3 ft 9 ins)
Weight	1365 kg (3009 lbs)
Front suspension	Double wishbone
Rear suspension	Double wishbone
Top speed	217 mph
0-60 mph	3.30 seconds

Silverstone - South Circuit

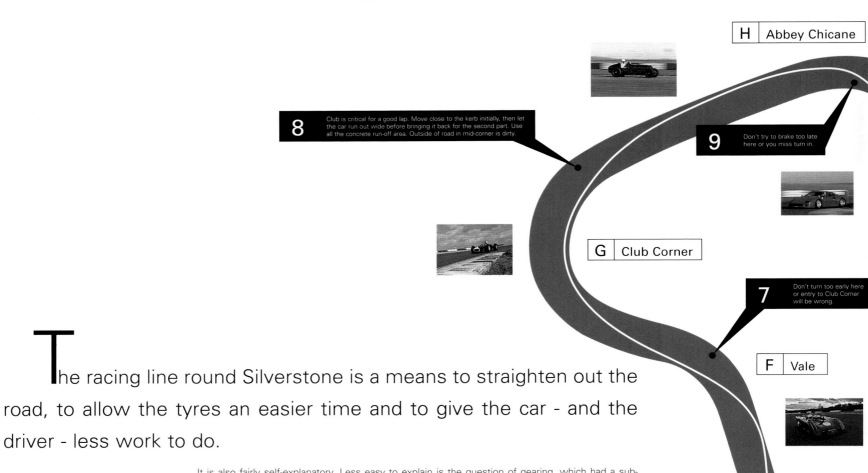

H | Abbey Chicane

8 Club is critical for a good lap. Move close to the kerb initially, then let the car run out wide before bringing it back for the second part. Use all the concrete run-off area. Outside of road in mid-corner is dirty.

9 Don't try to brake too late here or you miss turn in.

G | Club Corner

7 Don't turn too early here or entry to Club Corner will be wrong.

F | Vale

T he racing line round Silverstone is a means to straighten out the road, to allow the tyres an easier time and to give the car - and the driver - less work to do.

It is also fairly self-explanatory. Less easy to explain is the question of gearing, which had a substantial influence on the standing start performance figures tabulated on the following pages. Most of the cars in this book were intended for Le Mans, and were fitted with a hugely tall first gear.

In a 24-hour race the start is relatively unimportant and so first gear is usually put to another use like negotiating a hairpin. This makes the car impossible to get off the line quickly for a representative zero to 60 mph sprint. We have not included a top speed for much the same reason, because in most cases engineers would gear the car according to the length of the straight. This makes top speed as much an engineering exercise as a useful measurement. There were one or two cars, too, which ran out of room at Silverstone, but could have reached another number on the acceleration chart. You will also see how some very powerful cars were slow to get going, then extremely fast once they did. This was either gearing, or in some cases traction. If extra power only spins the wheels then the car doesn't accelerate.

The other comparative element was lap times. Here you see that cars which were either not very powerful or very quick to 60 mph were sometimes fast round the lap thanks either to light weight or the extra grip of slick tyres. In all cases we tested the cars exactly as they were so you should look at technical specs as well as the performance numbers.

E | Stowe Corner

6 Kerb on exit is smooth and grippy, use half of it.

Silverstone - South Circuit

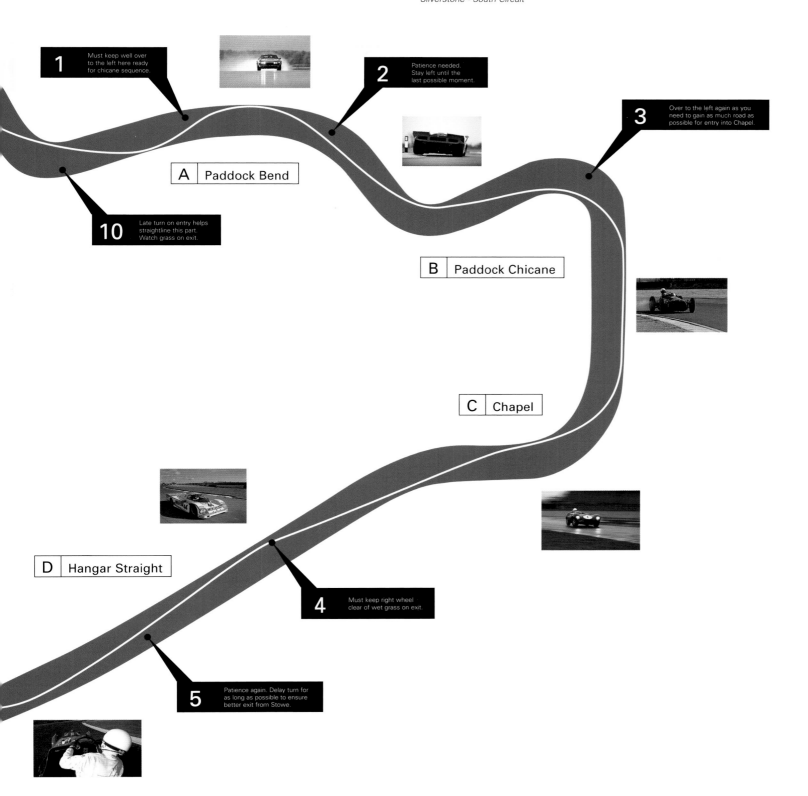

1 Must keep well over to the left here ready for chicane sequence.

2 Patience needed. Stay left until the last possible moment.

3 Over to the left again as you need to gain as much road as possible for entry into Chapel.

| A | Paddock Bend |

10 Late turn on entry helps straightline this part. Watch grass on exit.

| B | Paddock Chicane |

| C | Chapel |

| D | Hangar Straight |

4 Must keep right wheel clear of wet grass on exit.

5 Patience again. Delay turn for as long as possible to ensure better exit from Stowe.

Acceleration and lap times

MPH	Panhard B1	Bugatti T35B	Alfa Romeo 8C 2300	Aston Martin Ulster	ERA B Type	Frazer Nash Le Mans Replica	BRM V16 Mk 2	Jaguar D-Type	Maserati 250F	Maserati T61	Lotus 18	Ferrari 250GTO
10.00	2.8	1.0	0.6	1.5	0.5	1.4	0.8	1.3	0.6	0.7	0.8	0.9
20.00	6.5	2.0	1.9	2.5	1.5	2.3	1.2	2.5	1.4	1.5	1.5	1.7
30.00	16.4	2.9	3.6	4.9	2.2	3.5	1.6	3.5	2.3	2.2	2.2	2.6
40.00	36.4	3.8	5.0	6.1	3.0	4.6	2.0	4.4	2.9	2.9	2.9	3.8
50.00		5.1	6.5	9.0	3.8	6.7	2.7	5.3	3.5	3.7	4.0	5.3
60.00		6.0	9.4	13.8	4.8	8.9	3.9	6.3	4.3	5.8	4.5	6.5
70.00		7.6	13.9	16.9	6.0	12.2	4.7	7.7	5.1	5.9	4.6	8.1
80.00		9.0	18.7	24.9	7.3	15.5	5.6	9.2	6.2	6.9	5.2	9.8
90.00		11.9			9.1	19.5	6.7	10.9	7.3	8.0	6.1	11.4
100.00		14.8			11.0	25.5	7.9	12.9	9.2	9.7	7.5	14.2
110.00					14.3		9.1	15.9	10.7	11.6	12.1	
120.00							10.5		12.0	13.6		
130.00												
140.00												
150.00												
Lap Times	2m 43.0sec	1m 27.4sec	1m 36.5sec	1m 32.8sec	1m 21.8sec	1m 31.0sec	N/A	1m 20.3sec	1m 17.8sec	1m 17.2sec	1m 16.1sec	1m 20.9sec

TESTER'S NOTES

* Lap times for all but the Ferrari Enzo and Alfa Romeo TZ were recorded at Silverstone's original South Circuit. That has been revised for the 2010 Grand Prix season so the comparison is no longer available.
** The BRM V16 managed the acceleration runs, but developed a misfire every time we tried to lap Silverstone at speed.
*** The TZ and the Enzo were tested at Anglesey Circuit's 2.1-mile International layout in North Wales. These are cars' average lap speeds, for interest rather than comparison: TZ – 67 mph; Enzo (Pirelli tyres) – 75.4 mph.
For the purposes of comparison, a modern Audi RS4 Estate recorded a 72 mph average lap of Anglesey on a wet road.

Acceleration and lap times

	Alfa Romeo TZ	Ferrari 512S	Ferrari 365 GTB/4 Daytona	Porsche 935 K3	Ferrari 312T3	Ferrari 512 BBLM	Lola T297	Tyrrell 011	Ferrari F40	Porsche 962	McLaren F1 GTR	Ferrari Enzo	MPH
	0.9	0.2	0.9	1.4	0.4	0.5	0.6	0.4	1.0	0.8			10.00
	1.5	0.8	1.7	2.3	1.1	1.0	1.2	1.1	1.5	1.3			20.00
	2.8	1.4	2.4	3.5	1.3	1.9	2.1	1.4	2.0	1.9	1.8	1.4	30.00
	3.9	2.0	3.1	4.5	2.1	2.3	3.0	2.0	2.5	2.4	2.3	1.9	40.00
	4.8	2.4	4.4	5.3	2.5	4.1	3.7	2.6	3.0	2.9	2.7	2.7	50.00
	6.6	3.3	5.4	5.9	3.0	5.0	4.7	2.9	3.9	3.6	3.2	3.3	60.00
	9.0	3.9	6.5	6.4	3.7	6.5	5.6	3.6	4.7	4.6	3.9	3.9	70.00
	11.5	4.7	8.1	7.0	4.1	8.8	6.7	4.0	5.5	5.0	4.5	5.0	80.00
	15.0	5.6	9.7	8.0	4.7	9.9	7.8	4.5	6.6	5.9	5.6	5.7	90.00
	19.8	6.4	11.7	8.8	5.5	11.7	9.3	5.3	7.8	6.6	6.3	6.5	100.00
		7.7	14.3	9.6	6.7	14.4	11.0	6.2	8.9	7.3	7.2	7.4	110.00
		8.9		11.0	7.8	17.1	13.3	7.1	10.2	8.0	9.2	9.4	120.00
		10.6		12.2	8.9			8.2		10.0	10.4	10.9	130.00
										10.6	11.2	12.1	140.00
											12.8	14.0	150.00
	N/A	1m 08.2sec	1m 19.5sec	1m 07.6sec	1m 01.9sec	1m 12.1sec	1m 09.3sec	1m 02.2sec	1m 14.5sec	1m 04.0sec	1m 13.9sec	N/A	

	Engine capacity/config.	Engine position	Valve gear	Power	Power to weight ratio	Transmission	Tyre sizes
Panhard B1	*5114cc/4 cylinders in line*	*Front*	*Auto atmospheric inlet valves, camshaft-operated side exhaust valves*	*50 bhp @ 1400 rpm*	*45 bhp per ton*	*Rear drive, 4 speed and reverse, chain final drive*	*F: 875x105 R: 895x135*
Bugatti T35B	*2292cc supercharged/ 8 cylinders in line*	*Front*	*Single overhead camshaft*	*160 bhp @ 4500 rpm*	*210 bhp per ton*	*Rear drive, 4 speed and reverse, non-synchro*	*F: 500x19 R: 500x19*
Alfa Romeo 8C 2300	*2336cc supercharged/ 8 cylinders in line*	*Front*	*Twin overhead camshafts*	*155 bhp @ 5200 rpm*	*151 bhp per ton*	*Rear drive, 4 speed and reverse, non-synchro*	*F: 500x19 R: 600x19*
Aston Martin Ulster	*1495cc/4 cylinders in line*	*Front*	*Single overhead camshaft*	*85 bhp @ 5000 rpm*	*82 bhp per ton*	*Rear drive, 4 speed and reverse, non-synchro*	*F: 550x18 R: 550x18*
ERA B Type	*1488cc supercharged/ 6 cylinders in line*	*Front*	*Twin high cams, short pushrods & rockers*	*150 bhp @ 6500 rpm*	*203 bhp per ton*	*Rear drive, 4 speed and reverse pre-select*	*F: 550x16 R: 650x16*
Frazer Nash Le Mans Replica	*1971cc/6 cylinders in line*	*Front*	*Single high camshaft, short pushrods, cross-shaft rockers*	*140 bhp @ 5750 rpm*	*184 bhp per ton*	*Rear drive, 4 speed and reverse synchromesh*	*F: 550x16 R: 550x16*
BRM V16 Mk 2	*1490cc supercharged/ 16 cylinders in vee*	*Front*	*4 overhead camshafts*	*550-600 bhp @ 11500 rpm*	*904 bhp per ton*	*Rear drive, 5 speed and reverse, non-synchro, rear-mounted transaxle*	*F: 550x16 R: 700x16*
Jaguar D-Type	*3442cc/6 cylinders in line*	*Front*	*Double overhead camshafts*	*250 bhp @ 5750 rpm*	*252 bhp per ton*	*Rear drive, 4 speed and reverse synchromesh*	*F: 550x16 R:600x16*
Maserati 250F	*2493cc/6 cylinders in line*	*Front*	*Twin overhead camshafts*	*218 bhp @ 8000 rpm*	*346 bhp per ton*	*Rear drive, 5 speed and reverse, non-synchro, rear-mounted transaxle*	*F: 550x16 R: 650x16*
Maserati T61	*2890cc/4 cylinders in line*	*Front*	*Twin overhead camshafts*	*240 bhp @ 6500 rpm*	*400 bhp per ton*	*Rear drive, 5 speed and reverse, non-synchro, rear-mounted transaxle*	*F: 550x16 R: 650x16*
Lotus 18	*2495cc/4 cylinders in line*	*Mid*	*Twin overhead camshafts*	*250 bhp @ 7000 rpm*	*585 bhp per ton*	*Rear drive, 5 speed and reverse, rear-mounted transaxle*	*F: 500x15 R: 650x15*
Ferrari 250GTO	*2953cc/12 cylinders in vee*	*Front*	*Single overhead camshaft per bank*	*296 bhp @ 8000 rpm*	*283 bhp per ton*	*Rear drive, 5 speed and reverse, synchro gearbox*	*F: 600x15 R: 650x15*
Alfa Romeo TZ	*1570 cc/4 cylinders in line*	*Front*	*Twin overhead camshafts per bank*	*155 bhp @ 8000 rpm*	*246 bhp per ton*	*Rear drive, 5 speed and reverse, synchromesh*	*F: 500x15 R: 550x15*
Ferrari 512S	*4993cc/12 cylinders in vee*	*Mid*	*Twin overhead camshafts per bank*	*550 bhp @ 8500 rpm*	*654 bhp per ton*	*Rear drive, 5 speed and reverse, syncromesh transaxle*	*F: 110/235x15 R: 150/260x15*
Ferrari 365 GTB/4 Daytona	*4390cc/12 cylinders in vee*	*Front*	*Twin overhead camshafts per bank*	*405 bhp @ 8300 rpm*	*278 bhp per ton*	*Rear drive, 5 speed and reverse, synchromesh, rear-mounted transaxle*	*F: 215/700x15 R: 225/700x15*
Porsche 935 K3	*3211cc twin turbo chargers/6 opposed cylinders*	*Rear*	*Double overhead camshafts per bank*	*750 bhp @ 8200 rpm*	*773 bhp per ton*	*Rear drive, 4 speed and reverse, mid-mounted synchromesh transaxle*	*F: 280/610Rx16 R: 325/650Rx18*
Ferrari 312T3	*2992cc/12 cylinders horizontally opposed*	*Mid*	*Double overhead camshafts per bank*	*510 bhp @ 12,400 rpm*	*855 bhp per ton*	*Rear drive, 5 speed and reverse, non-synchro transverse transaxle*	*F: 920/220x13 R: 150/260x13*
Ferrari 512 BBLM	*4390cc/12 cylinders horizontally opposed*	*Mid*	*Double overhead camshafts per bank*	*400 bhp @ 7200 rpm*	*357 bhp per ton*	*Rear drive, 5 speed and reverse, synchromesh transaxle*	*F: 100/250x15 R: 110/270x15*
Lola T297	*1950cc/4 cylinders in line*	*Mid*	*Double overhead camshafts*	*290 bhp @ 9500 rpm*	*503 bhp per ton*	*Rear drive, 5 speed and reverse, non-synchro transaxle*	*F: 820/220x13 R: 140/230x13*
Tyrrell 011	*3000cc/8 cylinders in vee*	*Mid*	*Double overhead camshafts*	*500 bhp @ 11500 rpm*	*925 bhp per ton*	*Rear drive, 5 speed and reverse, non-synchro transaxle*	*F: 105/230x13 R: 150/260x13*
Ferrari F40	*2936cc/Twin turbo-chargers, 8 cylinders in vee*	*Mid*	*Double overhead camshafts per bank*	*478 bhp @ 7000 rpm*	*434 bhp per ton*	*Rear drive, 5 speed and reverse, synchromesh transaxle*	*F: 245/402Rx17 R: 335/352Rx17*
Porsche 962	*3164cc/Twin turbo, 6 opposed cylinders*	*Mid*	*Twin overhead camshafts per bank*	*670 bhp @ 8300 rpm*	*742 bhp per ton*	*Rear drive, 5 speed and reverse, synchromesh transaxle*	*F: 300/630Rx17 R: 325/680Rx17*
McLaren F1 GTR	*6064cc/12 cylinders in vee*	*Mid*	*Twin overhead camshafts per bank*	*600 bhp @ 7000 rpm*	*594 bhp per ton*	*Transverse, 6 speed and reverse, straight-cut gears*	*F: 275/35Rx18 R: 345/35ZRx18*
Ferrari Enzo	*5998 cc/12 cylinders in vee*	*Mid*	*Twin overhead camshafts per bank*	*650 bhp @ 7800 rpm*	*476 bhp per ton*	*6 speed, semi automatic*	*F: 245/35ZRx19 R: 345/35ZRx19*

NB. For imperial measurements see the individual technical specifications for each car.

Comparative technical data

Wheelbase	Track	Brakes	Length	Width	Height	Weight	Front suspension	Rear suspension	Top speed
2300 mm	F: 1370 mm R: 1420 mm	Rear only: foot operated contracting band; transmission handbrake	3580 mm	1680 mm	1600 mm	1102 kg	Beam axle, semi-elliptic springs	Beam axle, semi-elliptic springs	60 mph approx
2400 mm	F: 1400 mm R: 1400 mm	Rod, chain and cable-operated drum	3800 mm	1490 mm	1235 mm	762 kg	Beam axle, semi-elliptic leaf spring	Live axle, quarter-elliptic leaf spring	130 mph
2750 mm	F: 1380 mm R: 1380 mm	Rod-operated drums	4200 mm	1500 mm	1270 mm	1027 kg	Beam axle, semi-elliptic leaf spring	Live axle, semi-elliptic leaf spring	120 mph
2603 mm	F: 1435 mm F: 1435 mm	Cable-operated drum	3987 mm	1600 mm	1168 mm	1040 kg	Beam axle, semi-elliptic springs	Live axle, semi-elliptic springs	102 mph
2438 mm	F: 1333 mm R: 1219 mm	Rod-operated drum	3556 mm	1574 mm	1168 mm	738 kg	Beam axle, semi-elliptic springs	Live axle, semi-elliptic springs	135 mph
2451 mm	F: 1270 mm R: 1270 mm	Hydraulic drum	3530 mm	1422 mm	1041 mm	738 kg	Independent, lower wishbones, transverse leaf	Live axle, torsion bars and 'A' bracket	120 mph
2349 mm	F: 1371 mm R: 1346 mm	Hydraulic disc, 6 pot calipers front and rear	3873 mm	F: 1574 mm R: 1524 mm	1041 mm	636 kg	Independent, trailing arms, oleo pneumatic struts	De Dion, oleo pneumatic struts	165-170 mph
2298 mm	F: 1270 mm R: 1219 mm	Hydraulic discs with power assistance	3911 mm	1651 mm	820 mm	992 kg	Independent, double wishbones, torsion bars	Live axle, torsion bars, radius arms, 'A' bracket	170 mph
2280 mm	F: 1360 mm R: 1355 mm	Hydraulic drum	4343 mm	1473 mm	1054 mm	630 kg	Independent, double wishbones, coil springs	De Dion, transverse leaf spring	160 mph
2200 mm	F: 1250 mm R: 1200 mm	Hydraulic disc	3780 mm	1500 mm	916 mm	600 kg	Independent, double wishbones, coil springs	De Dion, twin radius arm, transverse leaf	145 mph
2270 mm	F: 1290 mm R: 1260 mm	Hydraulic disc	3560 mm	1490 mm	740 mm	427 kg	Independent, double wishbones, coil spring/damper units	Independent, top links, radius rods, coil spring/damper units	160 mph approx
2400 mm	F: 1351 mm R: 1346 mm	Hydraulic disc	4400 mm	1701 mm	1245 mm	1045 kg	Independent, double wishbones, coil springs	Live axle, radius arms, semi-elliptic springs	170 mph
2200 mm	F: 1300 mm R: 1330 mm	Hydraulic disc	3950 mm	1510 mm	1200 mm	650 kg	Independent, wishbones, coil springs	Independent, lower wishbones, coil springs	157 mph
2400 mm	F: 1518mm R: 1511mm	Hydraulic disc	4140 mm	1955 mm	990 mm	840 kg	Independent, double wishbones, coil spring/damper units	Independent, lower wishbone, top links, radius arms, coil spring/damper units	195 mph
2400 mm	F: 1490 mm R: 1475 mm	Hydraulic disc and servo assistance	4395 mm	1843 mm	1220 mm	1454 kg	Independent, unequal length wishbones, coil spring/damper units	Independent, unequal length wishbones, coil spring/damper units	180 mph+
2225 mm	F: 1445 mm R: 1630 mm	Hydraulic disc	4820 mm	1985 mm	1150 mm	970 kg	Independent, MacPherson struts, lower wishbones	Live axle, semi-trailing arms, coil spring/damper units	203 mph
2560 mm	F: 1620 mm R: 1559 mm	Hydraulic disc	4274 mm	2128 mm	1016 mm	596 kg	Independent, rocker arms, inboard coil spring/damper units	Independent, radius arms, parallel links, coil spring/damper units	190 mph approx
2500 mm	F: 1500 mm R:1519 mm	Hydraulic disc	4500 mm	1800 mm	1194 mm	1120 kg	Independent, double wishbones, coil spring/damper units	Independent, double wishbones, coil spring/damper units	188 mph approx
2330 mm	F: 1340 mm R:1340 mm	Hydraulic disc	3860 mm	1800 mm	792 mm	576 kg	Independent, double wishbones, coil spring/damper units	Independent, lower wishbone, top link, radius arms, coil spring/damper units	190 mph+
2720 mm	F: 1740 mm R: 1600 mm	Hydraulic disc	4190 mm	F: 1770 mm R: 1645 mm	950 mm	540 kg	Independent, double wishbones, pull rods, coil spring/dampers	Independent, parallel links, top rocker arm, coil spring/dampers	185-190 mph
2451 mm	F: 1595 mm R: 1610 mm	Hydraulic disc	4430 mm	1981 mm	1130 mm	1101 kg	Independent, twin wishbones, coil spring/damper units	Independent, twin wishbones, coil spring/damper units	201 mph
2771 mm	F: 1605 mm R: 1600 mm	Hydraulic disc	4800 mm	1998 mm	995 mm	902 kg	Independent, twin wishbones, coil spring/damper units	Independent, top rocker arms, coil spring/dampers, bottom links	240 mph
2718 mm	F: 1558 mm R: 1488 mm	Hydraulic disc	4367 mm	1900 mm	1090 mm	1021 kg	Double wishbones, co-axial coil springs	Double wishbones, co-axial coil springs	240.1 mph
2650 mm	F: 1660 mm R: 1650 mm	Hydraulic vented disc	4702 mm	2035 mm	1147 mm	1365 kg	Double wishbone	Double wishbone	217 mph

Circuit photography:
Simon Childs, John Colley, Mike Johnson and Paul Harmer

Thanks to

Ten Tenths:
Ray Boulter, John Dabbs, Dave Griffiths, Mike Hallowes, Charles Knill-Jones
and also Henry Brooks, Ian Douglass, Julia Grinter, Stella Jackson, Holly Mason and Steve Ward

Ecurie Bertelli: Derrick Edwards, Judy Hogg
and Andy Bell
Tony Birchenhough and Dorset Racing
Simon Draper
Ferrari SpA & Ferrari UK
Paul Grist
Rick Hall and Rob Fowler
Bob Houghton
Richard I'Anson and Michael Whiting
Paul Lanzante
Richard Lloyd
Tony Merrick and his team
Lord Edward Montagu and
The National Motor Museum

Doug Nye
Olympus Cameras
Steve O'Rourke
Duncan Ricketts
Tony Rudd
Burkhardt Von Schenk
Cedric Selzer
Peter Shaw
Tom Wheatcroft and The Donington
Collection
Barrie 'Whizzo' Williams
The British Racing Drivers Club and
the staff of the Silverstone, Donington and
Anglesey circuits for their help throughout

Timing: John Grist and Mark Hargreaves at Datron Technology
Memorabilia photography: Rod Shone and Paul Harmer
DAT recording: Roger Lindsay and Richard Nowell, engineered by Martin Bell and Roger Lindsay,
produced by Nick Mason

Picture credits
*Page 8 top left Peter Kredenser. Page 9 top left Ten Tenths Archive. Page 20 top right Ten Tenths Archive. Page 28
top right Ten Tenths Archive. Page 36 top right and front flap top Ten Tenths Archive/Centro di Documentazione
Storica Alfa-Romeo. Page 42 top and bottom Ten Tenths Archive. Page 50 top right Ten Tenths Archive/Sydney
Morning Herald. Page 50 bottom right Ten Tenths Archive/Logan, Birmingham. Page 56 top right LAT. Page 64 top
right Ten Tenths Archive. Page 72 top right Ten Tenths Archive. Page 79 top left Ten Tenths Archive. Page 80 top right
Ten Tenths Archive/P. Colle, Service Photographique du Journal L'Union. Page 84 bottom Dexter Brown.
Page 88 bottom right Ten Tenths Archive. Page 96 bottom right LAT. Page 104 top right Ten Tenths Archive. Page 112
top right Ten Tenths Archive. Page 120 top right and bottom right Ten Tenths Archive. Page 128 top right LAT. Page
134 top right and bottom right LAT. Page 142 bottom right LAT. Page 148 top right and bottom right LAT. Page 156
bottom right Ten Tenths Archive. Page 164 top right LAT. Page 170 top right Ferret Fotographics (Ted Walker). Page
170 bottom right Ten Tenths Archive. Page 178 top right and bottom right LAT. Page 188 top right Ten Tenths Archive.
Page 198 top right Ten Tenths Archive. Every effort has been made to contact copyright holders. If any omissions do
occur the publisher would be delighted to give full credit in subsequent reprints and editions.*